U·X·L

ENDANGERED SPECIES

3RD EDITION

U·X·L
ENDANGERED SPECIES

3RD EDITION

VOLUME 2

ARACHNIDS

BIRDS

CRUSTACEANS

INSECTS

MOLLUSKS

Julia Garbus
Noah Berlatsky
Kathleen J. Edgar, Project Editor

U·X·L
A part of Gale, Cengage Learning

GALE
CENGAGE Learning·

Farmington Hills, Mich • San Francisco • New York • Waterville, Maine
Meriden, Conn • Mason, Ohio • Chicago

GALE
CENGAGE Learning·

U•X•L Endangered Species, 3rd Edition

Julia Garbus and Noah Berlatsky

Project Editor: Kathleen J. Edgar

Acquisitions Editor: Christine Slovey

Contributing Editor: Elizabeth Manar

Rights Acquisition and Management: Amanda Kopczynski and Ashley Maynard

Composition: Evi Abou-El-Seoud

Manufacturing: Wendy Blurton

Product Design: Kristine A. Julien

For product information and technology assistance, contact us at
Gale Customer Support, 1-800-877-4253.
For permission to use material from this text or product,
submit all requests online at **www.cengage.com/permissions.**
Further permissions questions can be emailed to
permissionrequest@cengage.com

Cover photographs: © Orangutan by Stephen Meese, © Rothschild's Starling by Nagel Photography, and © Grand Cayman Blue Iguana by Frontpage, all Shutterstock.com.

While every effort has been made to ensure the reliability of the information presented in this publication, Gale, a part of Cengage Learning, does not guarantee the accuracy of the data contained herein. Gale accepts no payment for listing; and inclusion in the publication of any organization, agency, institution, publication, service, or individual does not imply endorsement of the editors or publisher. Errors brought to the attention of the publisher and verified to the satisfaction of the publisher will be corrected in future editions.

LIBRARY OF CONGRESS CATALOGING-IN-PUBLICATION DATA

Names: Garbus, Julia, author. | Berlatsky, Noah, author. | Edgar, Kathleen J., editor. | Gale (Firm)
Title: U X L endangered species / Julia Garbus, Noah Berlatsky ; Kathleen J. Edgar, project editor.
Other titles: Endangered species.
Description: 3rd edition. | Farmington Hills, MI : U-X-L, A part of Gale, Cengage Learning, 2016. | Includes bibliographical references and index.
Identifiers: LCCN 2015037374| ISBN 9781410332981 (vol. 1 : alk. paper) | ISBN 9781410332998 (vol. 2 : alk. paper) | ISBN 9781410333001 (vol. 3 : alk. paper) | ISBN 9781410332974 (set : alk. paper)
Subjects: LCSH: Endangered species--Juvenile literature.
Classification: LCC QL83 .G37 2016 | DDC 591.68--dc23
LC record available at http://lccn.loc.gov/2015037374

Gale
27500 Drake Rd.
Farmington Hills, MI 48331-3535

978-1-4103-3297-4 (set)
978-1-4103-3298-1 (vol. 1)
978-1-4103-3299-8 (vol. 2)
978-1-4103-3300-1 (vol. 3)

This title is also available as an e-book.
978-1-4103-3296-7
Contact your Gale sales representative for ordering information.

Printed in China
1 2 3 4 5 6 7 20 19 18 17 16

Table of Contents

VOLUME 2: ARACHNIDS, BIRDS, CRUSTACEANS, INSECTS, AND MOLLUSKS

Arachnids

Birds

Crustaceans

Insects

Mollusks

VOLUME 3: AMPHIBIANS, CORALS, FISH, PLANTS, AND REPTILES

Amphibians

Corals

Fish

Plants

Reptiles

Reader's Guide

U•X•L Endangered Species, 3rd Edition, presents information on endangered and threatened mammals, birds, reptiles, amphibians, fish, corals, mollusks, insects, arachnids, crustaceans, and plants. Its 242 entries were chosen to give a glimpse of the broad range of species currently facing endangerment. While well-publicized examples such as the polar bear, tiger, and giant sequoia are examined, so too are less conspicuous—yet no less threatened—species such as the Ganges River dolphin, Knysna seahorse, and golf ball cactus.

The entries are spread across three volumes and are divided into sections by classes. Within each class, species are arranged alphabetically by common name.

Each entry begins with the species' common and scientific names. A fact box containing classification information—phylum (or division), class, order, and family—for that species follows. The box also lists the current status of the species in the wild according to the International Union for Conservation of Nature and Natural Resources (IUCN) and the U.S. Fish and Wildlife Service (USFWS, which administers the Endangered Species Act). Finally, the box lists the country or countries where the species currently ranges.

Locator maps outlining the range of a particular species are included in each entry to help users find unfamiliar countries or locations. In most entries, a color photo provides a more concrete visualization of the species. Sidebar boxes containing interesting and related information are also included in some entries.

Each entry is broken into three sections:

- The information under the subhead **Description and biology** provides a general description of the species. This includes physical dimensions, eating and reproductive habits, and social behavior.

- The information under the subhead **Habitat and current distribution** describes where the species is found today, its preferred habitat, and, if available, recent estimates of its population size. Research studies are not conducted at regular intervals for some of these species, so 10 or more years may pass before new estimates become available.

- The information under the subhead **History and conservation measures** relates, if possible, the history of the species and the factors currently threatening it. Conservation efforts to save the species, if any are underway, are also described.

Included in each volume of *U•X•L Endangered Species, 3rd Edition*, is an overview of the history and current state of endangerment and its causes. It is followed by an explanation of the fact boxes and classifications used in the set and then a discussion of the International Union for Conservation of Nature and Natural Resources (IUCN) that includes a brief history of the organization, its current focus, and a brief explanation of the status categories in which the IUCN places imperiled species. The next section focuses on the Endangered Species Act (ESA), briefly examining its passage, purpose, implementation, status categories, and current state. A look at the changes in species' status from the 2nd to 3rd edition follows. Each volume also includes a **Words to Know** section that provides definitions of words and terms used in the set.

At the back of each book is a selection of **Critical Thinking Questions** that encourage reflection on the causes of endangerment and human efforts to protect wildlife. A **Classroom Projects and Activities** section follows, offering ideas for discussion and collaborative problem-solving.

A **Where to Learn More** section lists books, periodicals, websites, environmental organizations, and other resources such as movies and apps. The book listing is annotated. The environmental organizations list—a selected catalog of organizations focusing on endangered species—contains contact information and a brief description of each organization.

Finally, the volumes conclude with a cumulative index providing access to all the species discussed throughout *U•X•L Endangered Species, 3rd Edition*.

The scope of this work is neither definitive nor exhaustive. No work on this subject can be. The information presented is as current as possible, but the state of endangered species changes almost daily.

A note about the 3rd Edition

Since the publication of *U•X•L Endangered Species, 2nd Edition*, in 2004, the endangered or threatened status of many of the species included in these volumes has changed. Through the efforts of conservationists (people who work to manage and protect nature) and legislators, some of these species have recovered or have been assigned a less-threatened status (known as downlisting). The bald eagle, for example, listed as threatened under the ESA at the time of the *U•X•L Endangered Species, 2nd Edition*, has been removed from the list entirely and downlisted to "Least Concern" by the IUCN. The bald eagle population had plummeted, in part, because the powerful pesticide DDT weakened the shells of the birds' eggs. Listed as endangered in 1967, the U.S. national bird recovered after DDT was banned, its habitat was protected, and captive breeding programs were instituted. Other successes include the grizzly bear, the American bison, the black-footed ferret, and the Steller sea lion in the United States; the Iberian lynx in Europe; the African elephant; the markhor, a wild goat that is Pakistan's national animal; and three monkey species from Central and South America.

Along with successes, there have been serious setbacks. Other species previously listed have declined to the very brink of extinction. Several are familiar, such as the gorilla, endangered because of hunting and disease, and the northern white rhino, of which only three are known to remain. But less well-known or beloved species suffer equally, especially if their populations have always been small. For example, the mongoose lemur, a monkey-like animal native to several islands near the coast of Africa, has dropped from vulnerable to critically endangered status due to the destruction of its forest habitat for agriculture. Some more developed countries with stable, strong governments, such as the United States and Australia, may have ample resources to devote to conservation, whereas less economically developed and less stable countries and regions often lack such tools. Of the 24 species described in this book that have moved to a more threatened status since 2004, more than half are from such areas, including many from war-torn or impoverished regions of Africa.

U•X•L Endangered Species, 3rd Edition, cannot cover all threatened species worldwide, but 38 new species have been included in this edition to ensure that the situations of animals and plants worldwide—as they stand 12 years after the publication of *U•X•L Endangered Species, 2nd Edition*—are represented. New species described include the most familiar butterfly in the United States, the monarch, which is under consideration as an endangered species by the USFWS. The vibrant black-and-orange insect feeds on milkweed plants, which are becoming rare because of pesticide use. The new species presented reflect the diversity of the world's endangered creatures. There are mammals such as the okapi, birds such as the African penguin, arachnids such as the peacock tarantula, crustaceans such as the vernal pool tadpole shrimp, insects such as the Morrison bumblebee, mollusks such as the freshwater pearl mussel, amphibians such as the axolotl, fish such as the great hammerhead shark, plants such as the whitebark pine, and reptiles such as the bog turtle. Corals are included for the first time. These ocean invertebrates, animals without backbones, are moving toward extinction more rapidly than other animals such as amphibians, mammals, and birds.

Conservationists today face similar concerns to those described in *U•X•L Endangered Species, 2nd Edition*, many with more urgency. Some species described in this book, such as the saiga, the gray and Indiana bats, and the Wyoming frog, have declined in number because of disease. Scientists are working hard to understand the illnesses and develop ways to prevent them. The biggest reason for endangerment, however, continues to be habitat loss. Species as diverse as the Grand Cayman blue iguana, the giant catfish, the peacock tarantula, and Chapman's rhododendron, a flowering plant, have become endangered because people have logged forests, planted crops, grazed animals, built homes, dammed rivers, and engaged in other activities that destroyed these species' habitats. Habitat fragmentation, when development results in animals' living areas being broken up into smaller, separated areas, has threatened species such as the maned wolf, pygmy hippopotamus, and California tiger salamander.

The problem of commercial exploitation has nearly doomed some species included in these volumes. Animals such as the long-tailed pangolin and the great hammerhead shark are captured illegally and are then sold for food or because their bodies are thought to have medicinal properties. In the oceans, overfishing continues to threaten such species as the southern bluefin tuna. Bycatch—being caught by mistake in nets intended for other animals—threatens other species such as sea turtles and sawfish. Laws and treaties protecting species can help preservation efforts, as can educating local communities about the importance of species that share their environment. However, laws and education may not stop people driven by hunger from eating endangered animals, or those driven by poverty from capturing and selling them. Conservationists say that one of the best ways to conserve threatened species is to help local communities find new ways of surviving that do not endanger wildlife.

Since *U•X•L Endangered Species, 2nd Edition*, was published in 2004, scientists, authors, and the media are using new terms to describe the effects of human activity on the environment, although the changes these terms describe have been ongoing for many years. First, scientists have begun referring to our era as that of a sixth great extinction. All species become extinct eventually, at a natural rate of several species per year. Before the era of humans, the planet experienced five periods of mass extinctions, when most living species disappeared. But since 1900, extinctions have increased to more than 100 times the natural rate. This sixth wave, unlike the earlier five, is human-caused. The **Endangerment and Its Causes** section discusses the different ways human actions threaten animal and plant species. Another change in terminology is that since 2004, climate change has become increasingly evident and increasingly discussed. Several animal species described in this book, such as polar bears and corals, have already been harmed by climate change. Scientists predict that if people continue burning fossil fuels (oil, gas, and coal) at the current rate, many more species will be at risk of extinction by the end of the 21st century.

Since 2004, the realities of climate change and the sixth wave of extinction have demonstrated even more strongly than before that the fates of humans and other living species are inextricably interwoven. It is possible to take measures that rescue endangered species from the edge of extinction, prevent others from becoming threatened, and improve people's lives at the same time. These measures, however, require more than intense efforts to save particular animals. They call for people to reflect on how their actions affect not only other humans, but also the species with which we share our planet. And then these reflections must turn into actions that will improve not only the situations of today's people, animals, and other species, but the lives of those that will come in the future.

Acknowledgments

Special thanks are due for the invaluable comments and suggestions provided by the *U•X•L Endangered Species* advisory board:

> Ela-Sita Carpenter, Museum Educator, Maryland Science Center, Baltimore, Maryland
>
> Adam J. Eichenwald, Neighborhood Nestwatch Researcher; Atlanta Representative at Smithsonian Migratory Bird Center, Atlanta, Georgia
>
> Martha N. Mather, 6th grade science teacher, Kennewick School District, Kennewick, Washington
>
> Carrie Radcliffe, Restoration Coordinator and Safeguarding Database Manager, Atlanta Botanical Garden, Atlanta, Georgia; Mountain Bog Project Coordinator, Georgia Plant Conservation Alliance, Athens, Georgia; Consulting Botanist, Georgia Department of Natural Resources and U.S. Forest Service Southern Region

The U•X•L staff would also like to offer its profound thanks to Cinqué Hicks, Director, and Jamie Vidich, Operations Manager and Content Development Lead, of Bookbright Media for their invaluable contributions to this set. Their vision, skill, and enthusiasm are much appreciated.

Comments and suggestions

Cengage Learning welcomes your comments on *U•X•L Endangered Species, 3rd Edition*, and suggestions for species to be included in future editions of this work. Please write: Editors, *U•X•L Endangered Species, 3rd Edition*, 27500 Drake Rd., Farmington Hills, MI 48331-3535; call toll-free: 1-800-877-4253; fax: 1-877-363-4253; or send an e-mail via www.gale.com.

Endangerment and Its Causes: An Overview

Living organisms have been disappearing from Earth since the beginning of life on the planet. Most of the species that have ever lived on Earth are now extinct. Extinction and endangerment can occur naturally as a normal process in the course of evolution or as the result of a catastrophic event, such as the collision of an asteroid with Earth. Scientists believe some 65 million years ago, an asteroid struck near Mexico's Yucatán Peninsula, bringing about the extinction of almost 50 percent of plant species and 75 percent of animal species, including the dinosaurs. Scientists have identified five great extinction episodes in Earth's history before humans appeared on the planet. Although these five periods were marked by widespread, rapid extinction, species are continually disappearing; species become extinct at a rate of one to five species a year due to disease, competition among species, or natural climate change.

When humans became the dominant species on the planet, however, the extinction rate of other species began to increase dramatically. Especially since the 17th century, technological advances and an ever-expanding human population have changed the natural world as never before. At present, scientists believe extinctions caused by humans are taking place at 100 to 1,000 times nature's normal rate between great extinction episodes. Species are disappearing faster than they can be created through evolution. Therefore, the planet has entered a sixth wave of mass extinction that scientists believe is caused by human activity.

Because scientists have described and named only a small percentage of Earth's species, it is impossible to measure the total number of species endangered or going extinct. At least 1.9 million animal species and 450,000 plant species have been identified, but scientists say that possibly millions more have not yet been discovered. According to the International Union for Conservation of Nature and Natural Resources (IUCN), amphibians and corals are the animal groups at highest risk of extinction, with about 40 percent of each group threatened. About 25 percent of mammals and 13 percent of birds are at risk. Since 1980, birds and mammals as a whole have become slightly more endangered, the status of amphibians has dropped more sharply, and the outlook for corals has plummeted.

Humans are endangering species and the natural world primarily in three ways: habitat destruction, commercial exploitation of animals and plants, and the introduction of nonnative species into a habitat. Human activity has also accelerated climate change, which already threatens some species. Some experts state that if climate change continues at its current level, 25 percent of all species could be at risk by 2050.

Habitat destruction

The destruction of habitats all over the world is the primary reason species are becoming extinct or endangered. Houses, highways, dams, industrial buildings, and ever-spreading farms now dominate landscapes formerly occupied by forests, prairies, deserts, scrublands, and wetlands. For instance, 46,000 to 58,000 square miles (119,000 to 150,000 square kilometers) of forest each year are destroyed worldwide, the equivalent of 36 football fields each minute. Tropical rain forests, home to 50 percent of all animal and plant species, once occupied 6 million square miles (15.5 million square kilometers) worldwide. Now, only 2.4 million square miles (6.2 million square kilometers) remain.

Habitat destruction can be obvious, or it can be subtle, occurring over a long period of time without being noticed. Pollution, such as sewage from cities and chemical runoff from farms, can change the quality and quantity of water in streams and rivers. To species living in a delicately balanced habitat, this disturbance can be as fatal as the clear-cutting of a rain forest.

When remaining habitats are carved into smaller and smaller areas or fragments, species living in those smaller areas suffer. The fragments become crowded, with increased competition for scarce resources and space. Access to food and water may become limited. In search of such resources, animals may be killed while crossing roads or may venture into areas inhabited by people, causing conflicts with them. And, very importantly, habitat fragmentation limits access to mates. A smaller pool of mates reduces a species' genetic diversity, the number of different genes in a population. Genetic diversity plays a key role in the evolution and survival of living things, allowing a species a greater chance of adapting to changing environments and resisting disease.

Commercial exploitation

Animals have long been hunted by humans, not only for their meat but also for parts of their bodies that are used to create clothing, medicines, love potions, trinkets, and other things. Overhunting has caused the extinction of many species and brought a great many others to the brink. Examples include some species of whales, slaughtered for oil and baleen; the black rhinoceros, which is killed for its horns; and bluefin tuna, which are prized as a delicacy in Asia. Species that people find attractive or interesting, such as certain corals and arachnids, may become threatened in the wild as they are collected or captured for the pet or hobby trade.

Although international treaties outlaw the capture and trade of many endangered or threatened species, these laws are difficult to enforce, especially in countries that lack resources or a stable government. The smuggling of endangered species is a huge international business, estimated to be worth $10 billion to $20 billion a year. One reason people may hunt, capture, and trade endangered species is because they feel they have little economic alternative. So they may eat endangered animals for protein or capture and sell them as a livelihood.

Introduced species

Native species are those that have inhabited a given biological landscape for a long period of time. They have adapted to the environment, climate, and other species in that locale. Introduced or exotic species are those that have been brought into that landscape by humans, either accidentally or intentionally. In some cases, these introduced species may not cause any harm. They may, over time, adapt to their new surroundings and fellow species, becoming "native." Most often, however, introduced species seriously disrupt ecological balances. They compete with native species for food and shelter. Often, they prey on the native species, which may lack natural defenses against the intruders. They may also carry diseases that infect the native species or may take the resources that native species require for survival. When introduced species cause or are likely to cause harm to an environment, they are called invasive species. In the last 500 years, introduced plants and animals, including insects, cats, pigs, and rats, have caused the endangerment or outright extinction of hundreds of native species. In fact, more than 40 percent of threatened or endangered species are at risk because of invasive species.

Climate change

When humans burn fossil fuels, carbon dioxide is released into the air. This gas in the atmosphere creates a layer of insulation that stops Earth's heat from going into space. The more carbon dioxide in the atmosphere, therefore, the warmer Earth becomes. Since the 19th century, when the Western world became industrialized, the levels of carbon dioxide in the atmosphere have increased by 33 percent. Earth became 1.5°F (0.8°C) warmer from 1901 to 2012. Scientists estimate that Earth could warm anywhere from 0.5 to 8.6°F (0.28 to 4.78°C) over the next 100 years. This trend is referred to as global warming. A related term, climate change, refers to all major, long-lasting changes in climate, including global warming but also encompassing longer, more severe heat waves and changes in rainfall that lead to floods or droughts. These heat waves and rainfall changes are linked to increased levels of carbon dioxide and other gases in the atmosphere.

Climate change threatens many species in many ways. Warming temperatures in polar regions threaten animals that live or hunt on ice, such as polar bears. As melting sea ice causes sea levels to rise, these rising waters could engulf areas near the shore where animal and plant species live. Warmer ocean temperatures kill or weaken corals, while warmer temperatures on land can force animals to move to cooler areas or wake animals too early from hibernation. Droughts threaten many animals, especially amphibians, and plants. The effects of climate change on species can be direct; for example, the endangered Australian ant only emerges in cool weather. Or it can be indirect, threatening a species by disturbing the web of life in which the species exists. The blue whale, for instance, eats small sea animals called krill, which feed on algae that grow under sea ice. Rising temperatures have melted sea ice, reducing the algae population. This reduction in food supply has decreased the krill population by as much as 80 percent, which in turn could threaten the blue whale. Some scientists state that climate change has already contributed to the extinction of one species: the golden toad, a small, bright orange amphibian from Central America.

U•X•L Endangered Species *Fact Boxes and Classification: An Explanation*

Each entry in *U•X•L Endangered Species, 3rd Edition*, begins with a shaded fact box that contains the common name of the species, followed by its scientific name. The box lists the classification information for that species: phylum (or division), class, order, and family. It also lists the current status of that species in the wild according to the International Union for Conservation of Nature and Natural Resources (IUCN; see page xxix) and the Endangered Species List compiled under the U.S. Endangered Species Act (ESA; see page xxxi). (Note: For a listing of species whose status has changed since the publication of the 2nd edition, see page xxxv.) Finally, the box lists the countries or regions where the species is currently found and provides a locator map for the range of the species.

Classification

Biological classification, or taxonomy, is the system of arranging plants and animals in groups according to their similarities. This system, which scientists around the world currently use, was developed by 18th-century Swedish botanist (a scientist who studies plants) Carolus Linnaeus. Linnaeus created a multilevel system or pyramid-like structure of nomenclature (naming) in which living organisms were grouped according to the number of physical traits they had in common. The ranking of the system, going from general to specific, is: kingdom, phylum (or division for plants), class, order, and family. The more specific the level (closer to the top of the pyramid), the more traits shared by the organisms placed in that level.

Scientists currently recognize six kingdoms of organisms: Animalia (animals, fish, humans); Plantae (plants, trees, grasses); Fungi (mushrooms, lichens); Protista (bacteria, certain algae, other one-celled organisms having nuclei); Eubacteria (bacteria, blue-green algae, other one-celled organisms without nuclei); and Archaea (one-celled organisms found only in extreme environments such as hot or highly acidic water).

Every living organism is placed into one of these kingdoms. Organisms within kingdoms are then divided into phylums (or divisions for plants) based on distinct and defining characteristics. An example would be the phylum Chordata, which contains all the members of the kingdom Animalia that have a notochord (a rod, such as a backbone, that runs up an animal's back to support its body). Organisms in a specific phylum or division are then further divided into classes based on more distinct and defining characteristics. The dividing continues on through orders and then into families. Organisms that share a family often have the same behavioral patterns.

To further define an organism, Linnaeus also developed a two-part naming system—called binomial nomenclature—in which each living organism was given a two-part Latin name to distinguish it from other members in its family. The first name—italicized and capitalized— is the genus of the organism. The second name—italicized but not capitalized—is its species. This species name is an adjective, usually descriptive or geographic. Together, the genus and species form an organism's scientific name.

How similar organisms are separated by their scientific names can be seen in the example of the white oak and the red oak. All oak trees belong to the genus *Quercus*. The scientific name of white oak is *Quercus alba* (*alba* is Latin for "white"), while that of the red oak is *Quercus rubra* (*rubra* is Latin for "red"). In the past, scientists mainly took account of physical characteristics and behavior to group species together and give them scientific names. Now that scientists are able to compare species' DNA sequences, they also use this genetic information to classify species.

Each species or organism usually has only one scientific name under binomial nomenclature, which enables scientists worldwide who do not speak the same languages to communicate with each other about the species. However, as scientists learn more about species, they sometimes reclassify them based on new information. In such cases, a species will have a former name and a new name. Species can also end up with more than one name when scientists disagree about how they should be classified, with some scientists using one name and others preferring another. Alternate scientific names for a species are called "synonyms."

The scientific names provided for the species in *U•X•L Endangered Species, 3rd Edition*, are those used by the IUCN and the Endangered Species List. The Endangered Species List draws its taxonomic information from the Integrated Taxonomic Information System (ITIS). ITIS has also been consulted as a source for *U•X•L Endangered Species, 3rd Edition*, to determine accuracy of species' scientific names and taxonomies.

International Union for Conservation of Nature and Natural Resources (IUCN)

The International Union for Conservation of Nature and Natural Resources (IUCN), one of the world's oldest international conservation organizations, is a worldwide alliance of governments, government agencies, and nongovernmental organizations. It was established in Fontainebleau, France, on October 5, 1948. Working with scientists and experts, the IUCN tries to encourage and assist nations and societies around the world to conserve nature and to use natural resources wisely. As of December 2015, IUCN members represent 89 governments, 127 government agencies, and more than 1,000 nongovernmental organizations.

The IUCN has six volunteer commissions. The largest and most active of these is the Species Survival Commission (SSC). The mission of the SSC is to conserve biological diversity by developing programs that help save, restore, and manage species and their habitats. One of the many activities of the SSC is the production of the IUCN Red List of Threatened Species.

Available online, the IUCN Red List website has provided the foundation for *U•X•L Endangered Species, 3rd Edition*. The list presents scientifically based information on the status of threatened species around the world. Species are classified according to their existence in the wild and the current threats to that existence.

IUCN Red List categories

The IUCN Red List of Threatened Species places threatened plants, animals, fungi, and protists (organisms such as protozoans, one-celled algae, and slime molds) into one of nine categories:

- **Extinct:** A species that no longer exists anywhere around the world.

- **Extinct in the wild:** A species that no longer exists in the wild, but exists in captivity, in cultivation, or in an area well outside its natural range.

- **Critically endangered:** A species that is facing an extremely high risk of extinction in the wild.

- **Endangered:** A species that is facing a very high risk of extinction in the wild.

- **Vulnerable:** A species that is facing a high risk of extinction in the wild.

- **Near threatened:** A species that currently does not qualify as critically endangered, endangered, or vulnerable, but is close to qualifying or may qualify in the near future.

- **Least concern:** A species that has been evaluated but does not qualify as critically endangered, endangered, vulnerable, or near threatened because it is widespread or abundant.

- **Data deficient:** A species on which there is little information to assess its risk of extinction. Because of the possibility that future research will place the species in a threatened category, more information is required.

- **Not evaluated:** A species that has not been evaluated for inclusion on the list.

The IUCN updates its Red List assessments at least once per year, giving a new version number to each update. The trends shown in the 2015 report were not encouraging. As of its version 2015.2 Red List, the IUCN listed 11,877 threatened animals, 10,896 threatened plants, and 11 threatened species from the fungi and protist groups. Threatened species are those classified by the IUCN as critically endangered, endangered, or vulnerable. The number of threatened species on the IUCN Red List in 2015 is more than twice the number listed in 2000. However, many new species have been evaluated since 2000, which accounts for part of the increase. Cycads (palmlike plants found in tropical and subtropical regions) and amphibians are the two groups with the greatest percentage of threatened species in 2015. It is estimated that 63 percent of all cycads are threatened and 41 percent of all amphibian species are threatened.

Endangered Species Act

The Endangered Species Act (ESA) was passed by the U.S. Congress in 1973 and was reauthorized in 1988. The purpose of the ESA is to recover species around the world that are in danger of human-caused extinction. There are three basic elements to the ESA program: the creation of a list of endangered animals and plants (the Endangered Species List), the formulation of recovery plans for each species on the list, and the designation of critical habitat for each species listed. Through this program, the act seeks to provide a means of conserving those species and their ecosystems.

The U.S. Fish and Wildlife Service (USFWS), a part of the Department of the Interior, is the federal agency responsible for listing (or reclassifying or delisting) endangered and threatened species on the Endangered Species List. The National Marine Fisheries Service is responsible for many species that live in the oceans. The USFWS website hosts the Environmental Conservation Online System (ECOS), which lists all the species on the Endangered Species List as well as related scientific reports. ECOS has provided crucial source material for *U•X•L Endangered Species, 3rd Edition.*

The decision to list a species is based solely on scientific factors. Once a species is placed on the list, the USFWS is required to develop a plan for its recovery and to designate critical habitat for the species. Critical habitat is an area that has been deemed essential to the physical and biological needs of the species, either in their original range or an area similar to it. The designated critical habitat must provide appropriate space for population growth and normal behavior so that a species may recover. Critical habitat designation does not prohibit human activity or create an isolated refuge for the species in the chosen area. Once it has been established, however, any federal agencies planning to build on that land (a highway, for example) must seek the permission of the USFWS. Any other activities requiring federal permits must go through the USFWS as well. Private landowners are not affected, except that the designation alerts the public to the importance of the area in the species' survival. The ESA explicitly states that the economic interests of the human community must be given ample consideration in designating critical habitats and requires the balancing of species protection with economic development.

When a species is placed on the Endangered Species List, it is positioned in one of two categories:

- **Endangered:** A species that is in danger of extinction throughout all or a significant part of its range.
- **Threatened:** A species that is likely to become endangered in the foreseeable future.

The ESA outlaws the buying, selling, transporting, importing, or exporting of any listed species. Most important, the act bans the taking of any listed species within the United States and its territorial seas. "Taking" is defined as harassing, harming, pursuing, hunting, shooting, wounding, cutting, trapping, killing, removing, capturing, or collecting. The taking of listed species is prohibited on both private and public lands.

Violators of the ESA are subject to heavy fines. Individuals can face up to $100,000 in fines and up to one year's imprisonment. Organizations found in violation of the act may be fined up to $200,000.

On November 2, 2015, there were 2,246 species on the Endangered Species List. This total included 1,345 animals and 901 plants. The total also included 1,592 species found on U.S. territory or in U.S. waters, while the remaining 654 were species found in other countries.

Since its passage in 1973, the ESA has been continually targeted by its many opponents. Some of those opponents believe the ESA prohibits human progress, placing the rights of other species ahead of the rights of humans. There are many interest groups who lobby against the ESA: building and real estate development associations oppose the ESA because it could present some federal impediments to the large financial gains to be made in constructing new communities or facilities. Loggers, oil companies, farmers, fishers, hunters, fur traders, and others whose means of making a living are affected are also heavily represented in anti-ESA activism. Politicians, even those who nominally support the ESA, do not often find it politically advantageous to provide the necessary support and funding to rescue little-known animals or to oppose large and powerful companies.

In 1995 many Texans became upset on hearing news reports that said the USFWS might designate millions of acres of Texas land as critical habitat for the golden-cheeked warbler, an endangered bird. Designation of critical habitat is a required step for every species listed under the ESA. As a result of public outcry, U.S. senator Kay Bailey Hutchinson, a Republican from Texas, helped pass legislation that halted the USFWS's activities in the entire United States. The USFWS was prevented from designating new endangered or threatened species or designating critical habitat for existing species for a year. According to the USFWS, far less land was being proposed as critical habitat than news reports suggested, and critical habitat designation has no effect on private landowners anyway, a fact that the public often overlooks. When the moratorium (suspension of activity) was lifted in 1996, the agency faced delays and a backlog of proposed species to address.

In 2011 the nonprofit Center for Biological Diversity (CBD) concluded 10 years of lawsuits against the USFWS. The CBD had argued that the government agency was acting too slowly in listing new species. Under the eight years of President George W. Bush's administration (2001–2009), only 62 new species were listed, compared to 522 listed under the previous eight years during President Bill Clinton's administration (1993–2001). Meanwhile, the list of proposed species was getting longer as the USFWS took its time in making decisions. When the CBD and the USFWS made a settlement in 2011, the government agency agreed to decide on the backlog of 757 candidate species by 2018.

As recently as 2015, President Barack Obama's administration proposed making major changes to the ESA that would give states a larger role in the process of proposing new species for the ESA. It would also require that species be proposed only one at a time, rather than in bunches, which is currently done and saves time and steps. Opponents say that these changes will make it harder for citizens and organizations to propose new species as endangered.

Some of the species included in *U•X•L Endangered Species, 3rd Edition*, are losing the last few acres, streams, caves, or hillsides they require to survive; others stand only a few individual animals away from extinction. In the meantime, government agencies, wildlife organizations, politicians, and individuals often disagree on how best to balance the needs of humans and endangered species. Human activities are frequently the cause of endangerment, and human interests often conflict with those of other species. However, there are many examples in *U•X•L Endangered Species, 3rd Edition*, that illustrate how human efforts, including the protections of the ESA, can be critical in bringing species back from the verge of extinction.

Changes in Status from the 2nd Edition

Key: PE = Proposed Endangered; OFF = Delisted because of recovery;
LR–CD = Lower Risk, Conservation Dependent; TH = Threatened;
R = Rare (no longer used); NT = Near Threatened; VU = Vulnerable;
EN = Endangered; CE = Critically Endangered;
EW = Extinct in the Wild

Species that moved to a less threatened status, 2004–2016

Mammals

Armadillo, giant: EN to VU (IUCN)

Bat, gray: EN to NT (IUCN)

Bison, American: EN to TH (ESA)

Bison, European: EN to VU (IUCN)

Elephant, African: EN to VU (IUCN)

Ferret, black-footed: EW to EN (IUCN)

Lynx, Iberian: CE to EN (IUCN)

Markhor: EN to NT (IUCN); EN to TH (ESA)

Marmoset, white-eared: EN to VU (IUCN)

Monkey, Central American squirrel: EN to VU (IUCN)

Panda, red: EN to VU (IUCN)

Rat, giant kangaroo: CE to EN (IUCN)

Sea lion, Steller: EN to NT (IUCN)

Tamarin, golden lion: CE to EN (IUCN)

Birds

Booby, Abbott's: CE to EN (IUCN)

Cormorant, Galápagos: EN to VU (IUCN)

Words to Know

Adaptation: A genetically determined characteristic or inherited trait that makes an organism better able to cope with its environment.

Alpine: Relating to mountainous regions.

Arid: Land that receives very little rainfall annually and has a high rate of evaporation.

Biodiversity: The entire variety of life on Earth.

Biologist: A person who studies living organisms.

Botanist: A scientist who studies plants.

Brackish: A mixture of freshwater and saltwater; briny water.

Browse: A method of grazing in which an animal eats the leaf and twig growth of shrubs, woody vines, trees, and cacti.

Canopy: The uppermost spreading, branchy layer of a forest.

Captive breeding: A practice by which biologists (people who study living organisms) help a species reproduce in a controlled environment, such as a zoo, aquarium, or captive-breeding facility. Humans carefully select mating partners based on the individuals' genetics, behavior, and age, to find a match that will produce the healthiest offspring.

Carapace: A shell or bony covering on the back of animals such as turtles, lobsters, crabs, and armadillos.

Carnivore: An animal that eats mainly meat.

Carrion: The decaying flesh of dead animals.

Cetacean: An aquatic mammal that belongs to the order Cetacea, which includes whales, dolphins, and porpoises.

Chaparral: An ecological community of shrubby plants adapted to long, dry summers and natural forest-fire cycles, generally found in southern California.

Clear-cutting: The process of cutting down all the trees in a forest area at one time.

Clutch: A number of eggs produced or incubated at one time.

Competitor: A species that may compete for the same resources as another species.

Conservation: The management and protection of the natural world.

Conservationist: A person who works to manage and protect nature.

Convention on International Trade in Endangered Species of Wild Fauna and Flora (CITES): An international agreement by 143 nations to prohibit trade of endangered wildlife.

Critical habitat: A designated area considered necessary for the protection and preservation of a species that has been listed under the Endangered Species Act (ESA) in the United States. The area, either within the species' historical range or in an area similar to it, must provide an environment for normal behavior and reproduction so that the species may recover. The critical habitat designation does not prohibit human activity or create a refuge for the species. Once it has been established, though, any federal agencies planning to build or conduct activities within that area must seek the permission of the U.S. Fish and Wildlife Service (USFWS). The designation also serves to alert the public to the importance of the area in the species' survival.

Crustacean: A shellfish, such as a shrimp or crab, that has several pairs of legs and a segmented body with a hard outer shell.

Deciduous: Shedding seasonally; for example, a tree whose leaves fall off annually or a forest made up of trees that shed their leaves annually.

Deforestation: The loss of forests as they are rapidly cut down to produce timber or to make land available for agriculture.

Desertification: The gradual transformation of productive land into land with desertlike conditions.

Diurnal: Active during the day.

Domesticated: Animals trained to live with or be of use to humans.

Ecosystem: An ecological system, including all of its living things and their environment.

Ecotourism: Tourism, usually to a scenic natural place, that aims to raise awareness of threats and minimize environmental damage to the place.

Endangered: A classification indicating that a species is in danger of extinction in the foreseeable future.

Endangered Species Act (ESA): The legislation, passed by the U.S. Congress in 1973, which protects listed species.

Endangered Species List: The list of species protected under the U.S. Endangered Species Act.

Endemic species: A species native to, and found only in, a certain region.

Estivate: To hibernate (or sleep) through the summer.

Estuary: Coastal waters where a freshwater river empties into a saltwater sea or ocean.

Extinct: Refers to a species or subspecies that no longer exists because all of its living members have died.

Extirpated species: A species that no longer survives in the regions that were once part of its range.

Fauna: The animal life of a particular region, geological period, or environment.

Feral: An animal that has never been domesticated or has escaped from domestication and has become wild.

Fledge: When birds grow the feathers needed for flight.

Flora: The plants of a particular region, geological period, or environment.

Forage: To search for food.

Fragmentation: The breaking up of habitat into smaller areas that no longer border each other.

Gene: The basic biological unit of heredity that determines individual traits. Part of the DNA molecule, the gene is transmitted from parents to children during reproduction, and contains information for making particular proteins, which then make particular cells.

Genetic diversity: The variety of genes that exists among all the individuals of a particular species.

Gestation: Pregnancy.

Habitat: The environment in which specified organisms live.

Herbivore: An animal that eats mainly plants.

Hibernate: To spend the winter in an inactive state.

Historic range: The areas in which a species is believed to have lived in the past.

Hybrid: An animal or plant that is the offspring of two different species or varieties, resulting in a genetic mix.

Inbreeding: The mating or breeding of closely related individuals, usually within small communities. Inbreeding occurs when both parents have at least one common ancestor.

Indicator species: Plants or animals that, by their presence or chemical composition, give some distinctive indication of the health or quality of the environment.

International Union for the Conservation of Nature and Natural Resources (IUCN): An international conservation organization that publishes the IUCN Red List of Threatened Species.

Introduced species: Flora or fauna not native to an area, but introduced from a different ecosystem.

Invasive species: Species from a different ecosystem that cause harm when they are introduced into a new environment.

Invertebrate: An animal without a backbone.

Larval: The immature stage of certain insects and animals, usually of a species that develops by complete metamorphosis.

Lichen: A plantlike composite consisting of a fungus and an alga.

Marsupial: Mammals, such as the kangaroo and the opossum, whose young continue to develop after birth in a pouch on the outside of the mother's body.

Metamorphosis: A change in the form and habits of an animal during natural development.

Migration: The act of changing location (migrating) periodically, usually moving seasonally from one region to another.

Molting: The process of shedding an outer covering, such as skin or feathers, for replacement by a new growth.

Monogamous: Having just one mate for life.

Native species: The flora or fauna indigenous or native to an ecosystem, as opposed to introduced species.

Naturalist: A person who observes nature to find its laws.

Nocturnal: Most active at night.

Old-growth forest: A mature forest dominated by long-lived species (at least 200 years old), but also including younger trees; its complex physical structure includes multiple layers in the canopy, many large trees, and many large, dead, standing trees and dead logs.

Overhunting: Too much hunting of a particular species, resulting in a decline in the population of the species, which can lead to endangerment or extinction.

Perennial: A plant that lives, grows, flowers, and produces seeds for three or more continuous years.

Plumage: The covering of feathers on a bird.

Poaching: Illegally taking protected animals or plants.

Pollution: The contamination of air, water, or soil by the discharge of harmful substances.

Population: A group of organisms of one species occupying a defined area and usually isolated from similar groups of the same species.

Predator: An animal that preys on others.

Prehensile: Adapted for grasping or holding, especially by wrapping around something.

Pupal: An intermediate, inactive stage between the larva and adult stages in the life cycle of many insects.

Rain forest: A dense evergreen forest with an annual rainfall of at least 100 inches (254 centimeters); may be tropical (e.g., Amazon) or temperate (e.g., Pacific Northwest).

Range: The area naturally occupied by a species.

Recovery: The process of stopping or reversing the decline of an endangered or threatened species to ensure the species' long-term survival in the wild.

Reintroduction: The act of placing new members of a species into a habitat where that species had formerly disappeared.

Reserve: An area of land set aside for the use or protection of a species or group of species.

Rhizomatous plant: A plant having an underground horizontal stem that puts out shoots above ground and roots below.

Runoff: Water that drains away from the land's surface, such as after a heavy rain, bringing substances with it.

Savanna: A flat tropical or subtropical grassland.

Scavenger: An animal that feeds on carrion (dead animals) or scraps rather than hunting live prey.

Scrub: A tract of land covered with stunted or scraggly trees and shrubs.

Slash-and-burn agriculture: A farming practice in which forest is cut and burned to create new space for farmland.

Species: A group of individuals related by descent and able to breed among themselves but not with other organisms.

Steppe: Vast, semiarid grass-covered plains found in southeast Europe, Siberia, and central North America.

Subspecies: A population of a species distinguished from other such populations by certain characteristics.

Succulent: A plant that has thick, fleshy, water-storing leaves or stems.

Sustainable development: Methods of farming or building human communities that meet the needs of the current generation without depleting or damaging the natural resources in the area or compromising its ability to meet the needs of future generations.

Taproot: The main root of a plant growing straight downward from the stem.

Taxonomist: A biologist who classifies species on the basis of their genes, characteristics, and behavior.

Temperate: Characteristic of a region or climate that has mild temperatures.

Territoriality: The behavior displayed by an individual animal, a mating pair, or a group in vigorously defending its domain (territory) against intruders.

Trafficking: Dealing or trading in something illegal, such as protected animal and plant species.

Troglobite: A species that lives only in caves.

Tropical: Characteristic of a region or climate that is frost free, with temperatures high enough to support—with adequate precipitation—plant growth year round.

Tundra: A relatively flat, treeless plain in alpine, Arctic, and Antarctic regions.

Underbrush: Small trees, shrubs, or similar plants growing on the forest floor underneath taller trees.

Urban sprawl: The spreading of houses, shopping centers, and other city facilities through previously undeveloped land.

U.S. Fish and Wildlife Service (USFWS): A federal agency that oversees implementation of the Endangered Species Act.

Vegetation: Plants or the plant life of an area.

Vulnerable: A classification indicating that a species satisfies some of the risk criteria for endangerment, but not at a level that warrants its identification as endangered.

Wetland: A permanently moist lowland area such as a marsh or a swamp.

Wildlife biologist: A person who studies living organisms in the wild.

Arachnids

Harvestman, Bee Creek Cave
Texella reddelli

PHYLUM: Arthropoda
CLASS: Arachnida
ORDER: Opiliones
FAMILY: Phalangodidae
STATUS: Endangered, ESA
RANGE: USA (Texas)

Harvestman, Bee Creek Cave
Texella reddelli

Description and biology

Harvestmen are eyeless spiders. They are often called daddy longlegs because they have small rounded or oval bodies to which four pairs of long, slender legs are attached. The Bee Creek Cave harvestman's body is orange or light yellowish-brown in color and measures only 0.07 to 0.1 inches (0.17 to 0.25 centimeters) long.

This harvestman is a slow-moving, predatory species. It grasps its prey with its pedipalps (pronounced PEH-duh-palps; special appendages located near its mouth). Its diet includes tiny, hopping insects called collembolans.

Biologists (people who study living organisms) have no information on the mating habits of this species. Young Bee Creek Cave harvestmen are white to yellowish white in color.

The no-eyed big-eyed wolf spider, also known as the Kauai cave wolf spider, is native to Hawaii. COURTESY OF GORDON. C. SMITH, U.S. FISH AND WILDLIFE SERVICE.

with which to inject and subdue its prey with its venom (poison). The no-eyed big-eyed wolf spider's usual food is the Kauai cave amphipod, a tiny crustacean (shellfish) that lives in the same caves as the spider. The two species have a predator/prey relationship: the amphipod gets its nutrients from the rotting vegetation (plants) on the moist rocks of the humid cave environment, and the spider then feeds on the amphipod.

Females of this species lay only 15 to 30 eggs in a clutch (number of eggs produced at one time). They carry the egg sac inside their mouths until the eggs hatch. At that time, fully developed and unusually large infant spiders emerge. The newborn offspring stay with their mother for a few days, riding on her back, until they are ready to hunt on their own. The life span of an adult no-eyed big-eyed wolf spider is at least six months.

Habitat and current distribution

The no-eyed big-eyed wolf spider inhabits only the deep areas of Koloa caves, located on the southeast coast of Kauai Island in the Hawaiian Islands. The spider is found in the caves as well as in small cavities attached to the cave that humans cannot reach.

In its extremely limited cave ecosystem (an ecological system including all of its living things and their environment), the no-eyed big-eyed wolf spider requires specific conditions. The humidity in the cave must be a constant 100 percent, the air must be stagnant (still), and the air temperature must be between 75°F and 80°F (24°C and 27°C). The caves must also have the right type of woody vegetation for the wolf spider's prey, the Kauai cave amphipod, to eat. The no-eyed big-eyed wolf spider is known to exist only in six caves in the Koloa area.

History and conservation measures

The no-eyed big-eyed wolf spider, along with its prey, the Kauai cave amphipod, were discovered in the beginning of the 1970s and for decades were believed to exist in only four caves. Two more caves with populations of the species were found in 2002. The species is limited to a small and very specific area and has become endangered because of the deterioration of its habitat. The caves in which these spiders live are located in a very popular and developed resort area of Hawaii. Tourism and urban growth are constant pressures. Water is already scarce in the region, and natural water sources have been diverted to meet the needs of nearby tourist facilities and urban areas. Without a constant supply of seeping water, the caves inhabited by the spider will dry out.

Runoff (water that drains away, bringing substances with it) from urban areas can pollute the groundwater with pesticides and other toxic (poisonous) chemicals. Runoff from nearby farms has already ruined the largest lava cave in the area: it became covered with waste residue from sugarcane production. Human visitors can also destroy these caves by trampling, littering, smoking, vandalizing, and altering the climate by merely entering the caves.

The no-eyed big-eyed wolf spider was given endangered status under the Endangered Species Act (ESA) in 2000, and the U.S. Fish and Wildlife Service (USFWS) completed a recovery plan for the species in 2006. The USFWS has determined a critical habitat area for the spider—an area considered necessary to the conservation of the species that requires special management and protection. The agency works with the owners of the land above the habitat to protect the caves where no-eyed big-eyed spiders are known to live, and its programs focus on protecting and improving the habitats in these caves. Scientists also believe that creating suitable habitats for the species in unoccupied caves will be important to help the species survive.

Spider, Tooth Cave
Neoleptoneta myopica

PHYLUM: Arthropoda
CLASS: Arachnida
ORDER: Araneae
FAMILY: Leptonetidae
STATUS: Data deficient, IUCN
Endangered, ESA
RANGE: USA (Texas)

Spider, Tooth Cave
Neoleptoneta myopica

Description and biology

The Tooth Cave spider is a very small, slender spider species. It measures just 0.06 inches (0.16 centimeters) long. Pale cream in color, it has relatively long legs. Because it lives in a dark cave environment, it has small, undeveloped eyes. A delicate predator, it feeds on tiny invertebrates (animals with no backbone).

Biologists (people who study living organisms) have no information on the spider's reproductive habits.

Habitat and current distribution

Tooth Cave spiders inhabit underground caves in limestone rock in the Edwards Plateau region in Travis County, Texas. There are only six caves where these spiders are known to exist. In these caves, the spiders are

*The Tooth Cave spider is only
known to exist in six caves.*
© DR. JEAN KREJCA.

usually found hanging from cave walls or ceilings by a single tangle or sheet web. In order to live, they require stable temperatures, high humidity, and a ready supply of small invertebrates on which to feed.

History and conservation measures

Not much is known about Tooth Cave spiders or other endangered cave invertebrates in the region because scientific studies were not undertaken there until the early 1960s.

The main threat to this spider is the loss of its habitat. Residential and urban areas continue to grow in this region. As a result, many caves have been paved over or filled in. Because the caves are formed by seeping water, any change or alteration in the flow of that water can change the environment of a cave. To meet the needs of these newly populated areas, much of this water has been diverted. Some caves have become dry while others have become flooded. Pollution from populated areas has also seeped into the groundwater, and the water in many caves has become contaminated.

Conservation efforts in Travis County, Texas, have focused on managing and setting aside land to protect the habitat of the Tooth Cave spider and seven other endangered species in the area. The county plans to have 30,428 acres (12,314 hectares) under conservation by 2016 in what is called the Balcones Canyonlands Preserve.

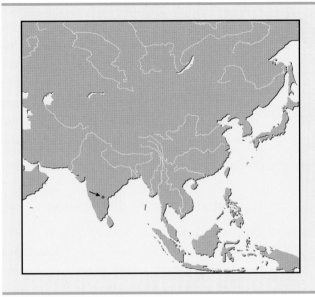

Tarantula, peacock
Poecilotheria metallica

PHYLUM: Arthropoda
CLASS: Arachnida
ORDER: Araneae
FAMILY: Theraphosidae
STATUS: Critically endangered, IUCN
Under consideration for
endangered status, ESA
RANGE: India

Tarantula, peacock
Poecilotheria metallica

Description and biology

The peacock tarantula is a large spider with a 6- to 8-inch (15- to 20-centimeter) leg span. Its hairy, segmented legs are a brilliant blue with a tiny dot of yellow. The carapace (hard upper shell of the front segment of the spider, pronounced CARE-a-pace) and abdomen (the bottom segment of the spider) are a less intense blue with a black-and-white pattern. Young spiders are a lavender color.

This tarantula species lives in deep hollows and cracks in large trees. It spins funnel-shaped webs, but it catches its favorite prey, flying insects, in flight and injects them with venom using its 0.75-inch (2-centimeter) fangs. A peacock tarantula's bite can cause humans severe pain but is not fatal. While flying insects, such as moths, seem to be its favorite prey, large spiders have also been known to prey on small lizards and mice. In captivity, the spider is typically fed grasshoppers and crickets.

To mate, a male tarantula deposits sperm on a web, picks it up with two appendages near its head called pedipalps (pronounced

Did You Know?

The peacock tarantula is threatened in the wild by collectors who illegally capture and sell these arachnids as pets. Such collectors threaten many other arachnid species as well, including tarantulas from Central America, South America, Africa, and at least five other species from India. The pet trade is not limited to arachnids. Rare birds, especially parrots, are commonly caught and sold illegally, as well as reptiles such as turtles, and many other types of live animals. Altogether, including the pet trade and trade in rhino horns and other animal products, the illegal wild animal trade is valued at around $10 billion a year.

The Internet has facilitated the trade in pets. Often sales of illegal pets are carried out fairly openly. Most of the trade is centered on Chinese websites, though eBay and Etsy are also used by illegal traders. Some progress has been made in restricting online sales, but the trade is far from being eliminated.

PEH-duh-palps), and then inserts the pedipalps into an opening on the female's abdomen. He then scurries away quickly before the female has a chance to eat him. After mating, females deposit 50 to 100 eggs into cocoon-like sacs. The young spiders hatch in 6 to 8 weeks, molting (shedding their skin) many times as they grow. Male peacock tarantulas live about 3 years, and females about 12 years.

Habitat and current distribution

The peacock tarantula has been found in only one subtropical old-growth forest (forest that has developed over a long period) in Andhra Pradesh, a state in southeastern India. Its range is less than 39 square miles (100 square kilometers). The total population is unknown.

History and conservation measures

This species was first discovered in 1899 in a railroad timber yard in an Indian town called Gooty. The Gooty tarantula, as it was then called, was not seen again until 2001, when it was rediscovered in a forest about 62 miles (100 kilometers) away from Gooty. This forest is the only place where these spiders have been found, so biologists (people who study living organisms) reasoned that the 1899 spider must have traveled to Gooty on a train.

The peacock tarantula inhabits an Indian "reserve forest," which is supposed to be protected, but it has been severely damaged by villagers who chop down trees for timber and firewood. If this destruction continues, this tarantula species could become extinct in the wild. Another threat is collection for the international pet trade (where it is often called a blue ornamental tree spider). Because the peacock tarantula is rare and beautiful, many tarantula fans want to own this species and will pay more than $500 for a female.

The peacock tarantula, found only in a small part of India, is threatened by both a decline of habitat and international pet traders, who capture the animal to sell for profit. © LINN CURRIE/SHUTTERSTOCK.COM.

Listed as critically endangered by the International Union for Conservation of Nature and Natural Resources (IUCN), the peacock tarantula was included on a 2012 list of the "100 most endangered species on the planet" put together by the IUCN and the Zoological Society of London. The U.S. Fish and Wildlife Service (USFWS) announced in 2013 that it would consider listing this species and 10 other similar tarantula species as endangered. (As of mid-2015, it had not made a decision.) If the USFWS does list the peacock tarantula, then the spider could no longer be imported legally into the United States.

Tarantula, red-kneed
Brachypelma smithi

PHYLUM: Arthropoda
CLASS: Arachnida
ORDER: Araneae
FAMILY: Theraphosidae
STATUS: Near threatened, IUCN
RANGE: Mexico

Tarantula, red-kneed
Brachypelma smithi

Description and biology

The red-kneed tarantula is one of the biggest spiders in the world, with a body length from 2.5 to 4 inches (6.4 to 10.2 centimeters) and a leg span of 4 to 7 inches (10.2 to 18 centimeters). It can weigh up to 2.5 ounces (71 grams). The tarantula's body is dark brown and covered in tiny hairs. The joints (knees) on its eight legs are bright orange and red, which is the basis for its name. It has two claws on the end of each of its legs for climbing and gripping. Although the red-kneed tarantula has eight eyes set above its mouth to give it forward and backward vision, it has very poor eyesight. It uses its sensitive leg hairs to feel its way about.

The red-kneed tarantula lives in a burrow it has dug out underground and lined with its spun silk. Its diet consists of centipedes and millipedes, beetles, crickets, grasshoppers, small frogs, lizards, and sometimes mice. It hunts at night, locating its prey by means of a special

The population of the red-kneed tarantula was first threatened when pet traders began exporting the animal from its habitat in Mexico. © APPSTOCK/SHUTTERSTOCK.COM.

sensitivity to its sounds and vibrations. The tarantula sits quietly, hidden in the dark, and then springs upon its victim. It grasps the prey with its two pedipalps (pronounced PEH-duh-palps; special appendages located near the mouth), and enfolds it with its eight legs and then bites it, injecting its venom. Tarantulas cannot digest food inside their own bodies; the venom they inject must serve two purposes. First, it stuns the prey into submission, and then it begins to digest the animal, turning its insides to liquid proteins and fats. The tarantula then sucks out the predigested liquid.

In late summer, male tarantulas look for females to mate. The male enters a female's burrow and then uses his pedipalps to inject sperm into the female's reproductive tract. He has to be very careful, though, because the female may attempt to kill and eat him. After mating, the female spins a web and lays anywhere from 50 to 700 eggs upon it. She then wraps the eggs in the silk ball and carries them between her fangs to incubate (keep warm until ready to hatch) for several weeks. Male tarantulas usually live about 8 years, while a female may live between 20 and 30 years.

Despite people's fears, red-kneed tarantulas are not as dangerous as they look. Although their bites are painful, they are generally not any more powerful than a bee sting. When threatened, red-kneed tarantulas display their red bristles and sometimes rub their back legs in order to drop hairs on their enemy. The hairs can cause rashes and even blindness. Even humans handling these spiders get rashes from their hairs. Generally, though, the red-kneed tarantula is not aggressive to humans. For this reason and because of its beautiful coloration, this tarantula became prized as a pet and has been one of the favored spiders for use in movies and television shows.

Habitat and current distribution

Red-kneed tarantulas can be found in deserts and rain forests. They are known to occur in southwestern Mexico, on the western faces of the Sierra Madre del Sur and Sierra Madre Occidental mountain ranges.

History and conservation measures

The friendliness to humans, brilliant coloring, and long life of the red-kneed tarantula have made the species very popular among spider collectors. Up until 1985, thousands of these tarantulas were imported from Mexico and then sold as pets. After years of this trade, the population of spiders in the wild declined, and in 1985 the Convention on International Trade in Endangered Species of Wild Fauna and Flora (CITES), an international treaty to protect wildlife, banned the exportation and importation of red-kneed tarantulas that have been caught in the wild. Only red-kneed tarantulas bred in captivity can be traded legally. This is the only species of tarantula to be protected under CITES.

The destruction of the red-kneed tarantula's natural habitat and the fact that many die before they reach reproductive age are major causes responsible for the decline in this species' population in the wild. In 2007 the Association of Zoos and Aquariums (AZA) initiated a species survival plan for the red-kneed tarantula. The AZA's involvement in captive breeding is expected to ensure the availability of the species for education programs and display.

Birds

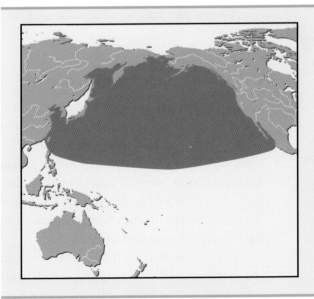

Albatross, short-tailed
Phoebastria albatrus

PHYLUM: Chordata
CLASS: Aves
ORDER: Procellariiformes
FAMILY: Diomedeidae
STATUS: Vulnerable, IUCN
Endangered, ESA
RANGE: Canada, China, Japan,
Mexico, Russia, South Korea, USA
(Alaska, California, Hawaii, Oregon,
Washington)

Albatross, short-tailed
Phoebastria albatrus

Description and biology

Albatrosses are ocean birds that spend most of their time gliding over the open sea. They come ashore only to nest. The short-tailed albatross, also known as Steller's albatross, is a large bird with a 7-foot (2-meter) wingspan. It has a white body, neck, and face. Its wings and the tip of its tail are dark brown. The bird feeds on fish, shrimp, and squid.

Like other albatrosses, the short-tailed albatross has an elaborate courtship ritual that includes dancing, stamping, and special greeting calls. After mating, the male and female build a crude nest in a clump of tall grass, and the female lays a single white egg. Both parents guard and incubate (sit on or brood) the egg for two to three months until it hatches. Both parents then feed the chick, often by regurgitating (vomiting) partially digested food directly into its beak. The young albatross leaves the nest at about five months of age but does not reach full maturity for eight to nine years. Short-tailed albatrosses mate for

Did You Know?

Albatrosses can remain at sea for as long as five years or more without touching land. They are also expert fliers. By using the winds and air currents, they can fly without flapping their wings for long periods. They come to land only for nesting, and they remain on land only long enough to produce and raise one chick. Albatrosses are not comfortable on land. Although they are skillful at flying, taking off and landing are not easy for them. They are particularly easy prey for hunters because they simply remain at their nests when the hunters approach.

There are 22 species of albatross, all of which are threatened or near threatened, according to the International Union for Conservation of Nature and Natural Resources (IUCN). Possibly the greatest threat to albatrosses is commercial long-line fishing (fishing with a line up to several miles long with a series of baited hooks along its length). About 100,000 albatrosses die each year from drowning after getting caught on baited hooks from fishing boats.

life. The couples return to the same nest sites year after year.

Habitat and current distribution

About 80 to 85 percent of all of the short-tailed albatrosses in the world mate and nest on the volcanic island of Torishima, one of the Izu Islands south of Tokyo, Japan. The species prefers level, open areas near tall clumps of grass. The bird's guano (feces) enriches the volcanic soil of Torishima, which in turn helps the growth of the tall grass clumps used as nesting sites.

The species' marine range covers most of the northern Pacific Ocean. The bird is most common along the coasts of Japan, eastern Russia, the Aleutian Islands, and coastal Alaska.

In the late 1940s biologists (people who study living organisms) estimated that there were fewer than 50 adult short-tailed albatrosses. By 2000 there were an estimated 1,200 birds in the wild. The population is believed to be increasing, with as many as 1,700 mature short-tailed albatrosses in existence worldwide as of 2012.

History and conservation measures

In the 19th century the short-tailed albatross had a population that numbered in the hundreds of thousands or millions. It nested on islands throughout the northwestern Pacific Ocean. Its range extended along the entire western coast of North America, where Native Americans hunted it for food.

By the early 20th century, its population had been quickly reduced by hunters seeking the bird's beautiful snowy-white breast feathers. In 1903 the Japanese government outlawed the hunting of the birds for their feathers, but the practice continued. Over a 17-year period in the late 1800s and early 1900s, it is estimated that feather hunters killed

The short-tailed albatross is the target of conservation efforts in the United States, Canada, and Japan, including breeding programs and protection from commercial fishing lines. © ALL CANADA PHOTOS/ ALAMY.

5 million of the birds. By 1929 only 1,400 birds remained in existence. In 1939 there was a volcanic eruption on Torishima, which buried much of the habitat. By the end of World War II (1939–1945), the short-tailed albatross was feared extinct. Then, in 1951, a tiny colony of 10 birds was discovered on Torishima.

Japanese biologists and conservationists (people who work to manage and protect nature) worked hard to save the short-tailed albatross. The Japanese island where the birds breed was declared a protected area and bird sanctuary in 1954. The habitat has been improved with new plantings and the elimination of feral animals (domestic animals that have become wild). The island is not inhabited by humans and permits are required to access it. Tourists may observe the island only from aboard ships.

The short-tailed albatross has made a significant recovery, moving from endangered to vulnerable status on the International Union for Conservation of Nature and Natural Resources (IUCN) Red List. The species remains in jeopardy, however. Its main breeding habitat is volcanic, and an eruption could destroy most of the albatross's habitat. A more common, and more critical, threat is the accidental death of birds that are caught in commercial fishing operations. Birds go after the bait in longline fishing (fishing with a line up to several miles long with a series of baited hooks along its length) operations and get snagged on fishing hooks. Commercial fishers in Alaska are being educated about the birds so that they will stop accidentally catching them.

Japan and the United States are developing a breeding colony of short-tailed albatrosses on Mukojima, a nonvolcanic island where the species used to nest that is about 218 miles (350 kilometers) south of Torishima. Chicks have been released at the island since 2008, and the population is monitored each year.

Blackbird, yellow-shouldered
Agelaius xanthomus

PHYLUM: Chordata
CLASS: Aves
ORDER: Passeriformes
FAMILY: Icteridae
STATUS: Endangered, IUCN
Endangered, ESA
RANGE: Puerto Rico

Blackbird, yellow-shouldered
Agelaius xanthomus

Description and biology

The rare yellow-shouldered blackbird is similar to its North American relative the red-winged blackbird. Its body is 7 to 9 inches (18 to 23 centimeters) long and dark gray in color. A distinctive yellow patch on its shoulder gives the bird its common name. Females are smaller than males. The bird eats mainly insects that it forages from plants and the leaves, branches, and bark of trees.

The birds nest in colonies and defend the immediate territory around their nests. Unlike many other blackbird species, the yellow-shouldered blackbird is monogamous (has just one mate for life). Mating usually takes place in April or May. The female lays 2 to 3 eggs and incubates (sits on or broods) them for 12 to 14 days before they hatch. After the nestlings are born, the female and male both share in gathering food.

The yellow-shouldered blackbird is threatened by the loss of its habitat in its native Puerto Rico. COURTESY OF MIKE MOREL, U.S. FISH AND WILDLIFE SERVICE.

There are two subspecies of yellow-shouldered blackbird: the Puerto Rico yellow-shouldered blackbird (*Agelaius xanthomus xanthomus*) and the Mona yellow-shouldered blackbird (*Agelaius xanthomus monensis*). Both subspecies are considered endangered.

Habitat and current distribution

Puerto Rico yellow-shouldered blackbirds nest in coconut palms and mangroves, most often near the coasts of and on offshore islets (very small islands) around Puerto Rico. It is found most often in the southwestern coastal areas of Puerto Rico. Approximately 900 of the Puerto Rico yellow-shouldered blackbirds exist on and around the island.

Mona yellow-shouldered blackbirds are found on the islands of Mona and Monito, which lie between Puerto Rico and Hispaniola (the large island located west of Puerto Rico and divided between Haiti on the west and the Dominican Republic on the east). These birds nest on the ledges or in the crevices of sheer coastal cliffs. In a 2007 survey of Mona and Monito islands, the U.S. Fish and Wildlife Service counted 260 Mona yellow-shouldered blackbirds.

History and conservation measures

The Puerto Rico yellow-shouldered blackbird was once abundant throughout coastal areas of Puerto Rico. It was found in various habitats, including freshwater wetlands (areas where there is a lot of water in the soil, such as swamps or tidal flats), open woodlands, and fields. In the 1970s its population was estimated at over 2,000.

Biologists (people who study living organisms) believe habitat destruction—mainly the draining of almost all the wetland areas in its range—was the initial cause of the bird's decline. The Puerto Rico yellow-shouldered blackbird continues to be threatened by mongooses, rats, and other mammals that eat its eggs. A more recent threat is the shiny cowbird. This bird, introduced to the region in the 1950s, slyly lays its eggs in the blackbird's nest. When the female blackbird returns, she broods (sits on to keep them warm) both her eggs and the cowbird's eggs. After the eggs hatch, the larger cowbirds dominate the smaller blackbirds, eating more of their food and often pushing them out of the nest.

The Mona yellow-shouldered blackbird is also currently threatened by habitat destruction (caused by increasing human development of Mona Island) and the shiny cowbird.

Controlling the cowbird population in the region and developing protected areas, such as Puerto Rico's Boquerón Commonwealth Forest, are among the measures conservationists (people who work to manage and protect nature) have undertaken to help the yellow-shouldered blackbird recover. A conservation program dedicated to the species that was established in 1982 has focused its efforts on installing artificial nests, monitoring the birds' reproduction, and controlling populations of the shiny cowbird, rats, and nest mites.

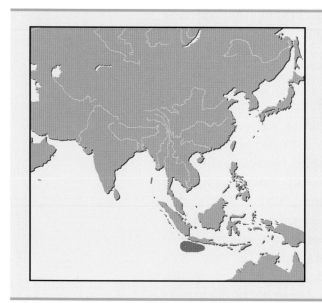

Booby, Abbott's
Papasula abbotti

PHYLUM:	Chordata
CLASS:	Aves
ORDER:	Suliformes
FAMILY:	Sulidae
STATUS:	Endangered, IUCN Endangered, ESA
RANGE:	Christmas Island

Booby, Abbott's
Papasula abbotti

Description and biology

Booby is the common name for a large seabird that inhabits tropical waters. Those members of the same family that inhabit temperate climates farther north or south are called gannets. The Abbott's booby measures about 31 inches (79 centimeters) long and weighs around 3 pounds (1.4 kilograms). It has a wingspan of almost 6 feet (1.8 meters). The female is slightly larger than the male. This booby is black and white in color and has a saw-toothed bill that is gray in males and pink in females. During greeting and courtship, the bird emits a distinctive deep, loud call.

The Abbott's booby is the only member of its family that builds its large, bulky nest at the top of a tall tree instead of on the ground. The female of the species lays one large, white egg between May and June. For about 56 days, both parents keep the egg warm by standing on it with their webbed feet. The chick grows slowly and does not fly until it is five or six months old. And only after about one year does the chick finally fly out to the open sea.

Like other boobies and gannets, Abbott's booby feeds on fish and squid. The bird dives after its prey from great heights and will often chase it underwater. Air sacs under the booby's skin help soften the impact when it hits the water; they also help the bird to float. The average life span for Abbott's booby is thought to be around 40 years.

Habitat and current distribution

Abbott's boobies nest only on Christmas Island (a territory of Australia), a tiny island in the Indian Ocean lying roughly 200 miles (320 kilometers) south of the island of Java (part of Indonesia). Biologists (people

Abbott's booby breeds only on Christmas Island in the Indian Ocean. Conservation efforts have been targeted at preserving its habitat, which is threatened by mining and other industrial development on the island. © ANT PHOTO LIBRARY/SCIENCE SOURCE.

who study living organisms) estimate that about 6,000 mature birds and 9,000 total birds exist.

The birds generally feed at sea northwest of the island.

History and conservation measures

Boobies were so named because of their rather dull facial expression and their extreme tameness. They are easily approached by humans, a factor that led to their early decline. Sailors and early settlers to the island could simply walk up to the birds and club them to death.

In the 20th century the main threat to Abbott's booby was the cutting down of the trees in which it nests. In order to mine mineral deposits, humans on Christmas Island removed the vast majority of the mature trees in the booby's habitat. Most of this tree removal ended by 1987. So much forest has been cleared, however, that the island's high winds threaten the boobies' nests and young in the remaining trees. A national park now covers most of the Abbott's booby's breeding area. Some areas that had been cleared for mining have been replanted with new trees; it is possible, however, that some forest clearing for mining could occur again in the future.

A continuing serious threat to the booby is the so-called yellow crazy ant (*Anoplolepis gracilipes*; called "crazy" because of its bizarre movements when disturbed). This ant, which is native to Africa, was accidentally introduced to Christmas Island early in the 20th century and has become widespread. The ants have wiped out the red crab population of Christmas Island. The red crab was essential to the ecosystem (an ecological system including all of its living things and their environment) because it ate weed seedlings and leaves, keeping the ecology of the rain forest in balance. Efforts to control the ants have been somewhat successful, but it is an ongoing battle. Finally, climate change poses an additional threat because warmer water could affect the supply of fish and squid that the booby needs to survive.

The Australian government is working to preserve this rare bird. The government's conservation plan includes controlling yellow crazy ants, studying and monitoring the birds and their habitat, working with mining companies to protect breeding habitat, and working to reduce climate change.

Bullfinch, Azores
Pyrrhula murina (also *Pyrrhula pyrrhula murina*)

PHYLUM: Chordata
CLASS: Aves
ORDER: Passeriformes
FAMILY: Fringillidae
STATUS: Endangered, IUCN
Endangered, ESA
RANGE: Portugal (Azores)

Bullfinch, Azores
Pyrrhula murina (also *Pyrrhula pyrrhula murina*)

Description and biology

The Azores (pronounced A-zawrz) bullfinch, also called the São Miguel bullfinch and known locally as the priolo (pronounced pree-OH-low), is a land bird native to the Azores archipelago, a group of nine islands plus some small islets (very small islands) in the North Atlantic Ocean about 800 miles (1,290 kilometers) off the coast of Portugal. The Azores bullfinch is in many ways like the common bullfinch that lives on the European continent. Some taxonomists (biologists who classify species on the basis of their genes, characteristics, and behavior) consider the Azores bullfinch to be a subspecies of the common bullfinch. The mainland bullfinch, however, has a bright red breast and gray back set off by a coal-black head, whereas the Azores bullfinch is dull in its coloring. Unlike the mainland birds, male and female Azores bullfinches are nearly identical in color. They can be identified by the white bars on their wings.

The Azores bullfinch faces threats to its habitat from deforestation and to its food supply from invasive plant species. © YULIA_B/ SHUTTERSTOCK.COM.

They are small in size, at about 6.25 inches (16 centimeters) long. Male Azores bullfinches are larger than females.

The Azores bullfinch lives in the laurel (a kind of evergreen tree) forests of the Azores. The bird's diet consists mainly of seeds. It eats the seeds of herbal plants in the summer, the seeds of fruits in the fall, and the seeds of trees and ferns in the winter. In the spring it eats flower buds. Because of this variety in its diet, the Azores bullfinch needs a good supply of specific plants in its area.

Habitat and current distribution

The Azores bullfinch can be found in dense laurel forests on the slopes of the Pico da Vara mountain on the island of São Miguel. The birds occupy an area of only about 32 square miles (83 square kilometers).

In 2008 biologists (people who study living organisms) estimated that about 1,300 Azores bullfinches were in existence.

History and conservation measures

In the 19th century there was an abundance of Azores bullfinches. Farmers viewed them as pests in their orchards and killed them whenever possible. The Azores government joined in the effort to eliminate the birds, in order to help the farmers with their crops, and actually paid rewards to local citizens who brought in bird beaks to prove they had killed the bullfinches. The campaign to get rid of the birds was highly successful. By the beginning of the 20th century, the Azores bullfinch had become quite rare.

For the few remaining Azores bullfinches, the introduction of foreign plants has caused another decline in population. The new plants have invaded the forests and overwhelmed the native plants. This forces the Azores bullfinches into smaller and smaller areas where the native vegetation (plant life) they eat and live in still exists.

In 1995 a local forestry program funded by the European Union was established to restore and expand laurel forests in the Azores in an effort to increase the population of the Azores bullfinch. A laurel forest on the slopes around the Pico da Vara summit was designated a natural forest reserve.

The protected Pico da Vara area was expanded in 2005 to cover about 24 square miles (61 square kilometers) of Azores bullfinch habitat. Additional conservation efforts include creating fruit tree orchards, removing nonnative plants, planting native species, and educating the local public and tourists about the Azores bullfinch's habitat and endangered status.

The population of the southern cassowary in Australia declined as a result of deforestation and development, while hunting posed the biggest threat to the species in Papua New Guinea and Indonesia.
© MAREK VELECHOVSKY/
SHUTTERSTOCK.COM.

Habitat and current distribution

Southern cassowaries live in the rain forests of northeastern Australia and the island of New Guinea, as well as on the Indonesian islands of Ceram and Aru. The Australian cassowary population was estimated to be about 2,500 mature birds as of 2010. New Guinea populations are less certain, although it is estimated that altogether the number of mature southern cassowaries is between 6,000 and 15,000 adults.

History and conservation measures

The southern cassowary is threatened by habitat loss in both Australia and New Guinea. Vehicle traffic also poses a threat to the birds. In New Guinea, cassowaries are hunted for food, and overhunting has eliminated cassowary populations in many areas. Industrial logging has also destroyed much cassowary habitat.

In Australia, conservation and management programs for the southern cassowary have been instituted, and much of the cassowary's current habitat is in protected areas. There has also been research into the effect of cyclones on cassowary populations because it is feared that global warming may increase severe weather in the future. In New Guinea, conservation efforts are needed to survey current populations and identify ways to protect cassowaries from logging operations and hunting.

Because of their role in seed dispersal, southern cassowaries are especially important for rain forest preservation. If cassowaries disappear, their whole habitat may be endangered.

Condor, California
Gymnogyps californianus

PHYLUM: Chordata
CLASS: Aves
ORDER: Accipitriformes
FAMILY: Cathartidae
STATUS: Critically endangered, IUCN
Endangered, ESA
RANGE: Mexico, USA (Arizona, California, Utah)

Condor, California
Gymnogyps californianus

Description and biology

The California condor, or California vulture, is the largest bird in North America and one of the largest flying birds in the world. It measures 45 to 55 inches (114 to 140 centimeters) long and weighs between 20 and 25 pounds (9 and 11 kilograms). It has a wingspan of up to 9.5 feet (2.9 meters), and its plumage (covering of feathers) is a dull gray black. A diamond-shaped white patch appears on the underside of its wings. The bird's neck and head are bare, and its skin color ranges from gray to orange red.

Like all vultures, the California condor feeds mainly on carrion (the decaying flesh of dead animals), preferring the carcasses of deer, cattle, or sheep. It will also attack and eat rodents, fish, and birds. When searching for food, the condor covers vast distances, sometimes as much as 140 miles (225 kilometers). It soars at speeds of 35 to 55 miles (56 to

The California condor, once extinct in the wild, responded to a captive-breeding program focused on conserving and increasing its population. © ANDY DEAN PHOTOGRAPHY/SHUTTERSTOCK.COM.

88 kilometers) per hour on warm thermal updrafts at altitudes up to 15,000 feet (4,570 meters). When not eating, the condor spends much of its time bathing and preening (smoothing feathers).

California condors do not begin breeding until they are between five and eight years old. Once paired, a male and female condor mate for life. Mating takes place during the winter, with the female laying one large egg. Both parents incubate (sit on or brood) the egg for 50 to 56 days until it hatches. The young condor fledges (develops flying feathers) within six months but may remain dependent on its parents for more than a year. Because of this, male and female pairs usually breed once every two years.

Habitat and current distribution

California condors prefer to nest in caves or on rocky cliffs in mountainous terrain and to roost (rest or sleep) on tall, exposed trees and rocky outcrops. They find food in nearby open savannas (flat, tropical or subtropical grasslands).

The species was considered extinct in the wild for a period of time, when in 1987 the last six wild California condors were taken into captivity. Over the next few years, conservation programs bred the California condor in captivity and carefully rereleased the birds in wild habitats, saving the species from total extinction. In 2000 there were 155 condors in existence, with 56 birds living in the wild. In 2014 there were 228 California condors in the wild. The California condor has been successfully reintroduced at sites in California, northern Arizona, and Baja California, Mexico. The Arizona birds also fly to and spend time in Utah.

History and conservation measures

Currently one of the rarest birds in North America, the California condor ranged over the entire continent for thousands of years. It fed on the remains of large Ice Age mammals such as mammoths and camels. Around 8000 BCE, when some of these mammals became extinct, the number of condors began to decline. By the time Europeans began colonizing North America in the 17th century, the bird's range was already reduced to the western coast and mountains. In the 19th century the condor population rapidly declined as settlers moved west. By the mid-20th century the birds numbered fewer than 100 and were restricted to a small area in central California. By the mid-1980s only five breeding pairs remained in the wild.

Many factors led to the California condor's decline. Because it feeds on the remains of other animals, it is susceptible to poisoning. Poisons ingested by animals become highly concentrated in the predators that eat them. Many condors die from eating the remains of animals that ingest pesticides or that are deliberately poisoned by farmers and ranchers. Others perish by eating lead bullets from the carrion of animals shot by hunters. Condors have also been hunted themselves and had their eggs stolen from their nests by collectors, both of which are illegal. As is the case with many other endangered species, the condor's habitat and feeding range has been reduced by human development.

Beginning in 1986 researchers decided to remove the remaining California condors from the wild and place them in captive-breeding programs. The condors bred well in captivity. In the early 1990s researchers started reintroducing captive-bred condors into the wild. Most of the birds released have slowly adapted to their new environment. In April 2002 the first baby condor born in the wild hatched from its shell in Ventura County. On May 1, 2002, the last wild condor taken into captivity back in 1987, a 22-year-old bird, was released back to the wilderness in Los Padres National Forest after spending 15 years in captivity and becoming the father of 16 baby condors. Scientists hoped that the released condors could remember enough about life in the wild to show the ropes to released condors that had been born in captivity.

The goal of the condor reintroduction program is to establish separate condor populations in the wild of at least 150 birds each. Despite its initial success, the program remains controversial. In hopes that the condors will stay in their sanctuary and not eat poisoned animals, biologists (people who study living organisms) often leave deer and cattle carcasses for the birds to eat. Some scientists and researchers believe this prevents the condors from surviving entirely on their own.

Steps have also been taken to reduce the threat of lead poisoning for California condors. The 2007 Ridley-Tree Condor Preservation Act requires the use of non-lead ammunition within the species' range in California. In addition, the Arizona Game and Fish Department and the California Department of Fish and Wildlife publish continuously updated lists of non-lead hunting ammunition, and Arizona has a program to provide free non-lead ammunition to hunters.

swims with its body almost entirely submerged in the water. Only its head and neck remain above the surface. When it spots its prey, the bird dives in a jackknife movement using powerful kicks to shoot through the water. The cormorant stays within about 650 feet (200 meters) of the shore when it swims.

Galápagos cormorants have a very elaborate courtship routine. Starting in the water, the male and female swim around one another in a kind of dance with their heads and necks held like a snake about to strike. They then go to shore, where they continue their routine. When the initial dance is over, the two birds build a nest of seaweed. Often the nest is situated within a colony of nests made by a dozen or more other Galápagos cormorant couples on hard-to-reach, sheltered rocky beaches or in lagoons. The male then begins to bring little additions for the nest to the female—"gifts" of more seaweed, dead starfish, or bits of litter, such as plastic bags, bottle caps, or rope. The female will add these gifts to the nest. Two or three eggs are then laid, usually in the spring, summer, or fall. The incubation period—during which both parents take turns sitting on the eggs to keep them warm—lasts about 35 days. Both parents initially take care of the young, but if there is enough food, the female will leave the male with the offspring (he will stay with the young for about nine months) and go off to find another mate. The female can breed as many as three times in one year.

Habitat and current distribution

The Galápagos cormorant lives on limited parts of the coastline of the Galápagos Islands off Ecuador, primarily in cold currents off the shores of Fernandina Island and off the northwestern shore of Isabela Island.

The total population was around 1,000 birds in the 1990s but then increased to nearly 1,700 birds by 2006. The rate of population growth seems to be slowing, so the population may be holding steady at its new, higher level.

History and conservation measures

Because there were originally no natural enemies of the Galápagos cormorant within its habitat, the bird had no need to fly and the species eventually lost the ability to do so. Instead, it developed its swimming skills. Humans eventually brought cats, dogs, and pigs onto the islands,

Did You Know?

In 1835 a young British naturalist (someone who observes nature to find its laws) named Charles Darwin visited the Galápagos Islands aboard the British ship H.M.S. *Beagle*. There, as he collected specimens of the abundant plant and animal life, he began to get the idea for his theory of evolution when he noticed that similar species were found on separate islands. The islands, with their thousands of species, were a particularly good place to study plant and animal life. With no human inhabitants on these islands until the 17th century, most animals on the islands lack the instinct of fear of humans. Although the islands were used by pirates and hunters during the 17th and 18th centuries, and small colonies were established there by Ecuador in the 19th century, most of the islands' current human population of 30,000 came later, in the 20th century.

Recognizing the extraordinary natural abundance of the Galápagos Islands, the Ecuadorian government turned 97 percent of the islands' area into a national park in 1959. In 1986 the waters around the islands were placed under protection as well. The government of Ecuador strengthened these protections in 1998, more than doubling the size of the marine reserve. Despite an active resource management campaign under the Charles Darwin Foundation, the islands have human-related conservation problems. Each year, 160,000 tourists come to the world-famous islands, and more and more people move to the islands because of the economic opportunities that the tourism industry provides. Such human activity has increased the number of feral animals (domestic animals that have become wild), introduced plants, and created illegal fisheries—all of which pose threats to the endangered species of the Galápagos Islands.

and feral populations (domestic animals that have become wild) developed. Suddenly the cormorant had predators on the islands. The birds were particularly ill equipped to protect themselves, because they had no fear of their enemies and they lacked the means to fly away from danger. Feral dogs in particular have drastically reduced the population in parts of its range.

Sea-cucumber fisheries have been established in the waters off the islands. (Sea cucumbers are sea animals prized as food in many Asian markets.) Although this fishing is legal in certain areas, fishers have been known to illegally collect sea cucumbers in areas that interfere with the cormorants' habitat. Pollution of many kinds has reached the islands, including an oil slick from the oil tanker *Jessica* that ran aground off the island of San Cristóbal in 2001, spilling hundreds of thousands of gallons of oil into the waters. Net fishing around the islands has been responsible for the deaths of individual birds that get caught in the nets, as well as for depleting their food supply from the waters.

The chicks leave the nest soon after hatching but remain with their parents until they fledge (develop flying feathers) at two to four months. Usually only one chick survives infancy.

Habitat and current distribution

The Siberian crane currently breeds in only two areas: in northeastern Siberia and in western Siberia. The northeastern population is the largest at about 3,500 birds, and it winters at or near Poyang Lake in eastern

The migratory Siberian crane has experienced a threat to its wetland habitats as projects such as China's Three Gorges Dam divert water for human use. © VISHNEVSKIY VASILY/ SHUTTERSTOCK.COM.

China. The western population now numbers fewer than 10 birds. The cranes stop at the Volga River delta in central Russia during migration and winter in northern Iran near the Caspian Sea. The birds may already be extinct in Afghanistan, India, Pakistan, and Turkmenistan, though there have been unconfirmed sightings in these countries.

The birds prefer to breed in marshy and lightly wooded tundra (plains in extremely cold climates) areas. In winter, they inhabit freshwater wetlands (areas where there is a lot of water in the soil, such as swamps or tidal flats) and shallow ponds.

History and conservation measures

Siberian cranes once nested throughout much of Siberia. Because the birds are seldom seen during migration, their wintering grounds remained a mystery until 1981, when the Poyang Lake site was discovered.

The major threat to the Siberian crane is hunting by humans along its migration path in Afghanistan and Iran. Habitat loss also puts the bird at risk. Wetlands along its migration routes and in its wintering regions have been drained by humans to create farmland and other developed land. In China, in addition to drainage for farmland, the wintering area in the mud flats around Poyang Lake has been impacted by the construction of the massive Three Gorges Dam on the Yangtze (Chang) River. Oil exploration and development is damaging the habitat in the breeding grounds in Siberia.

Programs have been established in the United States, Germany, and Russia to transfer eggs produced by Siberian cranes in captivity to wild sites, such as breeding grounds in the Tyumen region of western Siberia. In the wild, the eggs are hatched in electric incubators. Human keepers then care for the chicks until they fledge. To keep the cranes as isolated from humans as possible, the keepers dress in crane costumes. Captive-raised birds have been released in the Volga River delta to help maintain the western population.

The Siberian crane is protected by law in all countries in its range. A conservation project by the United Nations Environment Programme (UNEP) and the International Crane Foundation resulted in protection for more than 9,300 square miles (24,086 square kilometers) of the Siberian crane's habitat as of 2010. To ensure the species' survival, it will also be important to maintain and provide stronger protections in the Chinese wetlands along the birds' migration route and at Poyang Lake.

Crane, whooping
Grus americana

PHYLUM: Chordata
CLASS: Aves
ORDER: Gruiformes
FAMILY: Gruidae
STATUS: Endangered, IUCN
Endangered, ESA
RANGE: Canada (Northwest Territories, Alberta), USA (Florida, Louisiana, Texas, Wisconsin)

Crane, whooping
Grus americana

Description and biology

The whooping crane is so named because of its whooping, trumpetlike call. The tallest North American bird, it stands 5 feet (1.5 meters) tall and weighs almost 16 pounds (7.2 kilograms). It has an average wingspan of 7.5 feet (2.3 meters). This marsh or wetland bird has a snowy-white body, white wings marked with black tips, long dark legs, black feet, a red face, and a long, pointed yellow bill. Its diet consists of crabs, crayfish, frogs, rodents, insects, berries, and small birds.

The courtship behavior of whooping cranes is among the most unusual in nature. Their dance consists of strutting, leaping, head bobbing, wing flapping, and loud calls. Once a pair decides to mate, they mate for life. The pair requires a range of 300 to 400 acres (120 to 160 hectares) in order to find enough food and nesting sites.

In late spring, after building a nest on the ground among vegetation (plant life), a female whooping crane lays two light tan to green eggs.

Both parents incubate (sit on or brood) the eggs for about 30 days before they hatch. The chicks' feathers are cinnamon colored. They will not develop their white adult plumage (covering of feathers) until their second summer. Of the two chicks born, only one will survive to adulthood. The first-hatched chick (born one to two days ahead of the other) usually attacks and drives away the younger chick from the nest.

Habitat and current distribution

Whooping cranes are migratory (they relocate on a seasonal basis) birds. The only natural wild population breeds in the Wood Buffalo National Park on the border of the Northwest Territories and Alberta, in Canada. They begin migrating south in September in flocks of fewer than 10 birds. In November they arrive at their winter home in the Aransas National Wildlife Refuge in Texas on the coast of the Gulf of Mexico. In April they make the 2,600-mile (4,200-kilometer) trip back to Canada. The U.S. Fish and Wildlife Service (USFWS) estimated there were 310 whooping cranes in this wild population in 2015. There are also cranes reintroduced in Florida, Wisconsin, and Louisiana, numbering 132 total birds, and a captive population of 161 whooping cranes as of 2015.

The birds prefer to build their nests in wetlands (areas where there is a lot of water in the soil, such as swamps or tidal flats) and marshes. In winter, they inhabit coastal lagoons and fresh and brackish (mixture of freshwater and saltwater) marshes.

History and conservation measures

Scientists believe the whooping crane population was probably always small. They estimate that no more than 1,400 of these birds inhabited North America in 1870. Despite their small population, whooping

Did You Know?

With such a small population, the whooping crane probably would not survive without the help that humans provide, especially in breeding the birds. Captive breeding is a practice where biologists (people who study living organisms) help a species reproduce in a controlled environment, such as a zoo, aquarium, or captive-breeding facility. Humans carefully select mating partners based on the individuals' genetics, behavior, and age, to find a match that will produce the healthiest offspring.

The work does not stop there. The offspring must be reintroduced into the wild and learn to live on their own. Biologists also must make sure that there is enough protected habitat for the reintroduced species to call home. Captive breeding has helped many species come back from the verge of extinction, including the California condor, the American and European bison, and the golden lion tamarin in Brazil.

The whooping crane has seen its numbers increase because of conservation efforts and breeding programs. © KENT ELLINGTON/
SHUTTERSTOCK.COM.

cranes were found on the Great Plains and on both coasts of the United States. Before the American West was settled, they nested from Illinois to southern Canada and wintered from the Carolinas to Mexico.

By 1941, however, fewer than 20 whooping cranes existed in the world. Several factors contributed to their rapid decline. Many died as a result of hunting—for their meat or for sport. Others died from disease. The vast majority succumbed to habitat destruction. For example, over the past two centuries, more than half of all the wetlands that existed in the United States have been drained and filled in to create farmland, roads, and land suitable for homes and businesses.

Because each whooping crane couple requires a certain amount of territory, which they will defend from other whooping cranes, the population cannot grow unless they begin to use a different wintering ground. The Aransas reserve in Texas is only big enough to sustain a population of about 200 cranes. It is surrounded by developed communities, so it cannot be made larger.

In 1967 the USFWS began a whooping crane recovery program. Part of that program involved wildlife biologists (people who study living organisms in the wild) removing one of the two eggs from the birds' nests and placing them in the nests of sandhill cranes, which are closely related to whooping cranes. At first, the plan was successful. The sandhill cranes became "foster parents," incubating the eggs and then raising the whooping crane chicks as their own. However, when these whooping cranes grew to adulthood, they believed they were sandhill cranes and would not mate with other whooping cranes.

Biologists then began raising the captured eggs in captivity. Successful breeding programs were established in Maryland, Wisconsin, and Alberta, Canada. Beginning in 1993, captive-reared, nonmigratory whooping cranes were reintroduced to the wild on the Kissimmee Prairie in Florida. In the early 21st century programs were initiated that taught the reintroduced cranes to migrate by leading them in ultralight aircraft between Wisconsin and Florida. By 2012 there were populations of whooping cranes in Wisconsin, Florida, and Louisiana, though the Louisiana population is not migratory. To protect existing migratory whooping cranes, the USFWS's recovery program includes the conservation of wetlands and other suitable habitat in the bird's range.

Curlew, Eskimo
Numenius borealis

PHYLUM: Chordata
CLASS: Aves
ORDER: Charadriiformes
FAMILY: Scolopacidae
STATUS: Critically endangered, IUCN
Endangered, ESA
RANGE: Argentina, Brazil, Canada,
Chile, Paraguay, USA

Curlew, Eskimo
Numenius borealis

Description and biology

Curlews are large shorebirds. The Eskimo curlew is the smallest of the American curlews. It averages 11.5 to 14 inches (29 to 35.5 centimeters) in length. The feathers on its back are dark brown, while those on its breast are lighter. Its throat is almost white in color. The upper part of its breast and the underside of its wings are marked with dark brown streaks. Its legs are gray, and its eyes are dark brown.

Because of the fat layer it builds up for winter migration, the Eskimo curlew is also called the prairie pigeon or the doughbird. Its 2-inch (5-centimeter) black, curved bill is rich in nerve endings. When the bird sticks its bill in the ground to feed, these nerves detect vibrations caused by underground insects and worms. It also feeds on snails and berries.

Eskimo curlews begin breeding in May and June. A female lays 3 to 4 green-brown eggs in a nest of straw and leaves. The nest is hidden in a hollow in the ground. She then incubates (sits on or broods) the eggs for 18 to 30 days. After hatching, the young chicks are cared for by both parents until they fledge (develop flying feathers).

Habitat and current distribution

During breeding season, Eskimo curlews inhabit arctic tundra. In winter they are found in the pampas (partly grassy, partly arid plain) of central Argentina. While migrating northward, they visit the tallgrass prairies west of the Mississippi River.

Since the 1980s there have been no confirmed sightings of Eskimo curlews. Many wildlife biologists (people who study living organisms in the wild) consider the species to be extinct. If there are any Eskimo curlews remaining in the wild, the population is extremely low.

History and conservation measures

At the beginning of the 19th century, Eskimo curlews numbered in the millions. But intense hunting of the bird as it migrated quickly reduced its population. The conversion of pampas and prairies into farmland also reduced its habitat and food supply. By the early 20th century, it was thought to be extinct.

After sightings of Eskimo curlew flocks were reported in Canada and the United States in the 1980s, a recovery program was developed. Soon after, however, the sightings stopped. The last confirmed sighting of an Eskimo curlew was in 1987 in the Sabine Pass between Texas and Louisiana near the Gulf of Mexico. The bird is protected in the United States, Canada, and Argentina. Its breeding and wintering grounds

Did You Know?

Once a massively abundant species, the Eskimo curlew saw its population decimated by hunting over a 20-year period in the 1800s. The curlew, however, is not the only bird to have suffered in this way. The North American passenger pigeon was once the most abundant migratory bird in the world, moving in flocks of incredible numbers. Witnesses at the time said that a single flock could darken the sky for hours at a time. After a few decades of human hunters poisoning, burning, shooting, trapping, asphyxiating (killing by suffocation), and stabbing them, only a few were left. They went extinct when the last pigeon—a female named Martha—died in the Cincinnati Zoo in 1914. The passenger pigeon went extinct because humans believed nothing they did could harm such an abundant creature, and its loss helped spark the beginning of the first environmental movement.

A drawing of the Eskimo curlew that appeared in John James Audubon's Birds of America, *published between 1827 and 1838.*
© THE NATURAL HISTORY MUSEUM/ALAMY.

continue to be monitored for possible sightings. Hunters, who are likely to explore in areas where the bird may still exist, are urged not to disturb or kill any Eskimo curlews they may encounter.

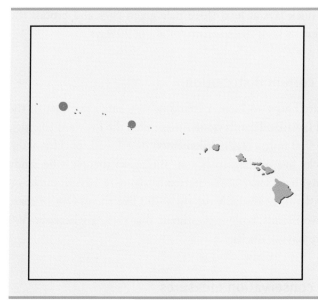

Duck, Laysan
Anas laysanensis

PHYLUM: Chordata
CLASS: Aves
ORDER: Anseriformes
FAMILY: Anatidae
STATUS: Critically endangered, IUCN
Endangered, ESA
RANGE: USA (Hawaii)

Duck, Laysan
Anas laysanensis

Description and biology

The Laysan duck is a relative of the more well-known mallard duck. An average Laysan duck measures 16 inches (41 centimeters) long. Its plumage (covering of feathers) ranges in color from light to dark brown. A white patch surrounds the duck's eyes and extends to its ear openings. The male (called a drake) has a green bill, while the female (called a hen or a duck) has a brown one. Both sexes have a purplish-green patch surrounded by white and black feathers on their secondary wings.

Relatively tame, the Laysan duck flies only short distances on the island it inhabits. During the day, it rests and forages on land for seeds and leaves. Tending toward being nocturnal (active at night), it feeds in lagoons on insects and their larvae.

The breeding season for Laysan ducks lasts from February to August. After building a nest on the ground within clumps of grass, a female Laysan duck lays at least three pale green eggs and broods the eggs (sits on them to keep them warm) for about 29 days.

Habitat and current distribution

Laysan ducks are native to Laysan Island, a very small member of the Northwestern Hawaiian Islands (sometimes called the Leeward Islands), located about 930 miles (1,495 kilometers) northwest of Honolulu. About 520 ducks live on Laysan Island. Biologists (people who study living organisms) have successfully started a colony of Laysan ducks on another small island, Midway. More than 400 live there. Out of these totals for the two islands, biologists estimate that there are between 500 and 680 mature Laysan ducks.

History and conservation measures

The Laysan duck population declined for two reasons. The first was human hunting for food and sport. The second—and more serious—was

The Laysan duck is one of several bird species native to Hawaii that is the target of conservation and protection programs. © IMAGE QUEST MARINE/ALAMY.

habitat destruction. At the beginning of the 20th century, rabbits were brought to Laysan Island. They quickly consumed most of the vegetation (plant life) on the island, destroying the ducks' nesting grounds. By the time the rabbits were eliminated from the island in the 1920s, the ducks had become almost extinct.

Laysan Island is a part of the Hawaiian Islands National Wildlife Refuge. Human access to the island is prohibited. The major threats to this species stem from bird diseases and natural disasters such as tsunamis. The small size of the bird population means that one such event can be extremely damaging; for example, in March 2011, an earthquake off the east coast of Japan caused a tsunami that killed half the duck population on Laysan Island.

Conservationists (people who work to manage and protect nature) are working to save this rare bird. They have improved the grassland and dunes on Laysan Island and established the birds on another island. The introduction of the duck to Midway has been successful, and conservationists plan to start colonies on other islands. Scientists will continue to monitor the birds and improve their habitat on all islands, as well as to begin captive-breeding programs followed by releasing the captive-bred ducks into the wild.

Because of disease, bad weather, lack of food, or lack of hunting experience, many eaglets do not survive their first year. Those that do survive may live 28 years or longer in the wild.

Habitat and current distribution

Bald eagles prefer to inhabit secluded forests with tall, mature trees and flowing water. Northern bald eagles usually migrate south during winter to open-water areas where food is abundant. The bald eagle ranges over most of the North American continent, from Alaska and Canada down to northern Mexico. Biologists (people who study living organisms) estimate that the total bald eagle breeding population comprises 250,000 individuals.

History and conservation measures

In 1782 the U.S. Congress adopted the bald eagle as the country's national emblem. However, this majestic bird began to disappear from the countryside as settlers destroyed its habitat in the American wilderness in the 19th and early 20th centuries. Western expansion also destroyed the great herds of bison, which were a major food source for the bald eagle, which fed on the bodies of dead bison. In addition, eagles were often shot by farmers and ranchers for threatening or preying on livestock. Hunters often found them a desirable trophy animal (an animal hunted for sport rather than for food) also.

By 1940 the number of bald eagles was so low that Congress passed the Bald and Golden Eagle Protection Act. This act made it illegal to kill, harass, possess (without a permit), or sell bald and golden eagles. Nonetheless, the eagle population continued to decline, especially after World War II (1939–1945). The cause of this population decline was eventually linked to widespread use of the powerful pesticide DDT (dichlorodiphenyltrichloroethane).

Farmers, foresters, and others used DDT to kill insects, rodents, and other pests that harmed agricultural crops and transmitted diseases. DDT does not break down chemically in the environment, however.

After being sprayed on cropland, it is washed (through rain and other precipitation) into nearby streams, rivers, and lakes. The DDT residue is absorbed by aquatic plants and small animals, which are then eaten by fish. In turn, the fish are eaten by bald eagles and other predators. At each step higher in the food chain, the DDT residue becomes more concentrated in the fatty tissues of the contaminated animals (a process called bioaccumulation).

The DDT poisoning caused the eggs of bald eagles (and other birds) to have thin, weakened shells. The eggs often broke during brooding or did not hatch at all, and the number of bald eagles quickly fell. By the early 1960s, only 417 pairs of nesting bald eagles existed in the lower 48 states. In some areas, they had disappeared completely.

In 1962 marine biologist Rachel Carson wrote *Silent Spring*. The book documented the dangers of pesticides, particularly DDT. A widespread public outcry resulted in most uses of DDT being banned in the United States by 1972.

This ban, coupled with efforts to protect bald eagle habitat, brought the bird back from near extinction. In July 1995 the U.S. Fish and Wildlife Service (USFWS) officially downlisted the bald eagle from endangered to threatened throughout the nation. By 2007 there were at least 9,789 nesting pairs of bald eagles in the contiguous United States (the connected 48 states), as well as at least 50,000 in Alaska, and the USFWS decided that the eagle could be removed from the Endangered Species List. The recovery of the bald eagle population is often cited as being among the greatest success stories in animal preservation and the U.S. conservation movement.

There are still threats to the bald eagle population, however, including collisions with motor vehicles and wind turbines, lead poisoning from hunters' shot (metal pellets) in carrion (the decaying flesh of dead animals) eaten by eagles, and destruction of nesting habitat. Nevertheless, once a rare sight, bald eagles are now commonly found nesting across North America.

The Philippine eagle is threatened by deforestation in its native country, where this has caused its population to decline. ©EDWIN VERIN/ SHUTTERSTOCK.COM.

Habitat and current distribution

The Philippine eagle is found on the Philippine islands of Leyte, Luzon, Mindanao, and Samar. Its primary habitat is rain forest. Biologists (people who study living organisms) estimate that between 90 and 250 pairs of Philippine eagles currently exist in the wild.

History and conservation measures

Hunting and trapping were the initial causes for the Philippine eagle's decline. Although these threats are still very real, deforestation (large-scale removal of trees) has become an even greater threat. The forests of the Sierra Madre, a mountain range on the northeastern coast of Luzon, provide the largest remaining habitat. Unless conservation measures are undertaken, logging of the forests will continue and the Philippine eagle's habitat will be destroyed.

A captive-breeding program for the Philippine eagle was established in 1987, and the first chick was hatched in captivity five years later. The Philippine Eagle Centre in Davao City, Mindanao, conducts the captive-breeding program, monitors the conservation of the populations in the wild, and is developing a reintroduction program to release the wild birds born in captivity. As of 2015, there were 36 eagles at the center, including 18 bred in captivity.

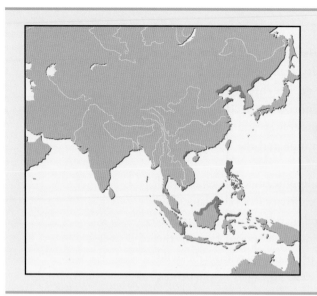

Egret, Chinese
Egretta eulophotes

PHYLUM: Chordata
CLASS: Aves
ORDER: Pelecaniformes
FAMILY: Ardeidae
STATUS: Vulnerable, IUCN
Endangered, ESA
RANGE: Brunei, China, Indonesia, Japan, Malaysia, North Korea, Philippines, Russia, Singapore, South Korea, Thailand, Vietnam

Egret, Chinese
Egretta eulophotes

Description and biology

Egret is the common name for herons that develop lengthy, drooping plumes during breeding season. The Chinese egret is a tall wading bird with long legs, a long neck, and a long, pointed bill. It measures 25 to 27 inches (63.5 to 68.5 centimeters) in height. Its plumage (covering of feathers) is pure white in color. A crest of white feathers forming a showy plume develops along the top and back of its head and neck.

The Chinese egret feeds alone or in small groups. It wades in shallow water to catch fish, shrimp, and crabs. Male and female egrets mate for life. After building a nest in a tree or in low vegetation (plant life), the female lays two to five eggs and incubates (sits on or broods) them for approximately 30 days until they hatch.

Habitat and current distribution

This species of egret breeds on small offshore islands along the western coast of China, North Korea, South Korea, and the eastern coast of Rus-

The Chinese egret, prized for its feathers in the 19th century, has seen its population decline in recent years because of industrial development and other disturbances to its habitat across eastern Asia.
© FLPA/ALAMY.

sia. It is also known to visit other islands and coasts along the South China Sea. Biologists (people who study living organisms) estimate that there are between 2,600 and 3,400 mature Chinese egrets worldwide.

The Laysan finch population in Hawaii is at risk of the effects of extreme weather conditions and climate change.
COURTESY OF THE U.S. FISH AND WILDLIFE SERVICE.

(sits on or broods) them for about 16 days. The young chicks fledge (develop flying feathers) in just over a month.

Habitat and current distribution

The Laysan finch is native to Laysan Island, an islet (very small island) of the Hawaiian Islands, located about 750 miles (1,200 kilometers) northwest of Niihau Island, as well as in the Pearl and Hermes Atoll, located about 930 miles (1,497 kilometers) northwest of Honolulu. The number of Laysan finches changes from year to year, and biologists (people who study living organisms) estimate that the population average (as of 2012) is about 5,000 birds.

On Laysan Island, the finches inhabit sand dunes around the coastline and a brackish (mixture of freshwater and saltwater) lagoon in the center of the island.

History and conservation measures

Early explorers to the region believed the Laysan finch's pleasing song made it an attractive cage bird. At the beginning of the 20th century, as many as 4,000 of these birds may have inhabited Laysan Island.

In 1903 rabbits were introduced to the island. They quickly ate most of the natural vegetation (plant life), destroying the habitat and food supply of the island's native birds. In 1909 U.S. president Theodore Roosevelt designated Laysan Island and other islands in the Hawaiian chain as part of the Hawaiian Islands Bird Reservation. However, this move did little to stop the decline of the Laysan finch population. In 1922 when the last rabbits were finally removed from the island, only about 100 of these finches remained. However, following the extermination of the rabbits, the Laysan finch population recovered well and quickly.

Although the numbers of Laysan finch do not appear to be declining, the species is still considered vulnerable. Laysan Island is part of the Hawaiian Islands National Wildlife Refuge. This limits the number of humans allowed to visit the island, providing further protection for the Laysan finch. Predator species such as rats, if accidentally introduced to the islands, could still easily wipe out the birds. Diseases carried by introduced birds could also destroy the finch population.

The primary threats to the Laysan finch are storms and drought, as well as global warming. Rising sea levels caused by climate change could threaten parts of Laysan Island, where the highest altitude is only 39 feet (12 meters) above sea level. Scientists also expect that, as average global temperatures rise, damage from hurricanes and droughts will also increase.

Flamingo, Andean
Phoenicoparrus andinus

PHYLUM: Chordata
CLASS: Aves
ORDER: Phoenicopteriformes
FAMILY: Phoenicopteridae
STATUS: Vulnerable, IUCN
Endangered, ESA
RANGE: Argentina, Bolivia, Chile,
Peru

Flamingo, Andean
Phoenicoparrus andinus

Description and biology

Flamingos are tall wading birds. They have long legs, a long curved neck, and distinctive pink plumage (covering of feathers). The birds move gracefully, whether walking or flying. The Andean flamingo stands 40 to 43.5 inches (102 to 110.5 centimeters) tall and weighs 4.4 to 5.3 pounds (2 to 2.4 kilograms).

The flamingo has a stocky bill that curves downward. Thin, flat membranes or gills line the rim of the bill. As the flamingo wades through marshes and lagoons, it scoops up muddy water with its bill and these membranes strain out food such as minute algae.

The flamingo's breeding season extends from December to February. Before mating, males and females undergo an elaborate courtship ritual, which they perform in unison. The female lays a single egg in a

The Andean flamingo saw its population decline in the 20th century because its eggs were collected for food and because of damage to its habitat by human activity. © PHOTOSHOT HOLDINGS LTD/ALAMY.

nest built out of mud into a cone 12 to 24 inches (30 to 61 centimeters) high and 12 inches (30 centimeters) wide. Both parents incubate (sit on or brood) the egg for 27 to 30 days. The chick often leaves the nest just 12 days after hatching. Sometimes, it is carried under one of its parents' wings.

Habitat and current distribution

As the names indicates, Andean flamingos are found in the Andes Mountains in the South American countries of Argentina, Bolivia, Chile, and

Did You Know?

Most years, strong winds on the Pacific Ocean near the equator flow west and push the ocean's warm surface water away from South America. Some years, the winds are weaker than usual or flow east toward South America, keeping the warmer ocean waters near the coast. South American fishers call the arrival of this warmer water and air El Niño, or "the (Christ) child" in Spanish, because it often started around Christmas.

The temporary climate shifts of El Niño affect people and animals all over the world. Some fish populations die and others are forced to migrate. In the case of the Andean flamingo, its chances for survival improve as the species is known to breed in parts of South America only in El Niño years.

Peru. They usually occupy salty lakes in mountainous areas at 7,545 to 14,760 feet (2,300 to 4,500 meters).

The Andean flamingo breeds at about 10 sites, including such salt lakes as Laguna Colorada in Bolivia, Laguna de Salinas in Peru, and Salar de Atacama in Chile. Breeding also takes place in Argentina in certain years. It is estimated that at least 28,000 Andean flamingos exist in the wild as of 2015.

History and conservation measures

The Andean flamingo once existed in great numbers. Now, this elegant bird is considered in jeopardy. As humans move deeper into its environment, this flamingo is threatened on many fronts. Human collectors steal its eggs. The body fat of the bird has historically been used as a rub to treat rheumatism, a disease of the joints. Mining operations pollute and destroy its habitat. Introduced wildlife species compete with it for food. Some, like the fox, prey directly on the bird. A long-term drought (lack of rain) in northern Chile that began in the early 1990s continues to take a huge toll on the population of the species. For these reasons, the Andean flamingo was given endangered status under the U.S. Endangered Species Act (ESA) in 2010.

Efforts were started in the 1980s to protect the known breeding grounds of the Andean flamingo. Conservation actions include preserving the Andean flamingo's habitats, preventing their eggs from being taken, and increasing public awareness of the species' endangered status.

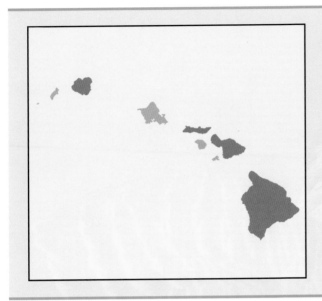

Goose, Hawaiian
Branta sandvicensis

PHYLUM: Chordata
CLASS: Aves
ORDER: Anseriformes
FAMILY: Anatidae
STATUS: Vulnerable, IUCN
Endangered, ESA
RANGE: USA (Hawaii)

Goose, Hawaiian
Branta sandvicensis

Description and biology

The Hawaiian goose or nene (pronounced NAY-nay) is uniquely colored. Its gray-brown feathers have white tips that form widely spaced bars on the bird's back. On its underside, the bars are closer together. The sides of the nene's neck are reddish brown with black-and-white markings. The bill, face, cap, and back of the neck are all black.

An average nene measures 22 to 30 inches (56 to 76 centimeters) long and weighs between 4 and 5 pounds (1.8 and 2.3 kilograms). The bird has excellent senses of hearing and sight. It also has strong legs and wings. It feeds mainly on vegetation (plant life), including grasses, leaves, herbs, and berries.

The breeding season for Hawaiian geese is from August to April. Male-female pairs (a male is known as a gander, a female as a goose) build nests on the ground, usually in a patch of vegetation. The female lays three to five eggs. Both the gander and goose incubate (sit on or

Grebe, Junín
Podiceps taczanowskii

PHYLUM: Chordata
CLASS: Aves
ORDER: Podicipediformes
FAMILY: Podicipedidae
STATUS: Critically endangered, IUCN
Endangered, ESA
RANGE: Peru

Grebe, Junín
Podiceps taczanowskii

Description and biology

Grebes are swimming birds that inhabit quiet waters around the world. They resemble both the loon (to which they are related) and the duck (to which they are not closely related). The Junín (pronounced hoo-NEEN), or Puna, grebe has a grayish-brown plumage (covering of feathers) on the top portion of its body. Its underparts and neck are white. An average Junín grebe measures 13 to 15 inches (33 to 38 centimeters) in length. It has a long neck and a fairly long, pointed bill. Its diet consists primarily of fish.

A male-female pair of Junín grebes breeds in patches of tall vegetation (plant life) in deep water. After breeding, they build a nest in a colony with other mating pairs on semi-floating vegetation beds. A colony consists of 8 to 20 nests, which are generally situated 3 to 13 feet (0.9 to 4 meters) apart.

A female Junín grebe usually lays two eggs between November and March. Biologists (people who study living organisms) have yet to learn how long it takes the eggs to hatch. After hatching, the young are carried by the male. This leaves the female free to dive to obtain food for herself and her young.

Habitat and current distribution

This species of grebe is found only on Lake Junín in the highlands of west-central Peru. Located at an altitude of 13,400 feet (4,084 meters), Lake Junín is a large, shallow lake bordered by extensive reed beds. During breeding season, the grebes forage (search for food) along the coast of the lake in open water. During the dry season, the birds move into the deeper central parts of the lake.

As of 2013 scientists estimated the Junín grebe population to be between 50 and 249 individuals, according to the International Union for Conservation of Nature and Natural Resources (IUCN).

History and conservation measures

At one time, several thousand Junín grebes inhabited Lake Junín. By the 1970s, the Junín grebe population was less than 400. It continued to drop steadily to a low of fewer than 50 birds in the early 1990s but then

The Junín grebe is found only at Lake Junín in Peru. © ALEJANDRO TABINI.

rebounded slightly. The bird remains in very risky circumstances and was given endangered status under the Endangered Species Act (ESA) in 2012.

The number of Junín grebes declined primarily because Lake Junín has become polluted by the poisonous runoff (water that drains away, bringing substances with it) from nearby copper mines. In addition, low water levels have had a negative effect on the bird's population. Water levels in the lake, which are regulated by a dam, regularly fluctuate by up to 6.5 feet (2 meters). The water supply is used both for mining activities and hydroelectric power. In some years water levels get so low that the marshlands at the edges of the lake dry up and the grebe loses its nesting habitat. Scientists have found that Junín grebes do not breed at all in such dry years. The low water levels also result in a scarcity of pupfish, the grebe's main food source.

Lake Junín is a Peruvian National Wildlife Reserve, where hunting and fishing are regulated. However, water continues to be drained periodically for mining and hydroelectric power operations. The Peruvian government passed a law in 2002 to restrict the amount of water that can be drained, but the law has not been enforced.

Plans to relocate Junín grebes to another lake have not been successful. Conservationists (people who work to manage and protect nature) state that a recovery plan for the species is urgently needed to prevent the Junín grebe's extinction. Experts believe that such a plan should educate the local people about the birds' needs, reduce pollution in Lake Junín, and improve the management of the lake's water level to benefit both wildlife and local people.

Ground-dove, purple-winged
Claravis godefrida (also *Claravis geoffroyi*)

PHYLUM: Chordata
CLASS: Aves
ORDER: Columbiformes
FAMILY: Columbidae
STATUS: Critically endangered, IUCN
RANGE: Argentina, Brazil, Paraguay

Ground-dove, purple-winged
Claravis godefrida (also *Claravis geoffroyi*)

Description and biology

The purple-winged ground-dove derives its common name from the three wide purple bars on its wings. The male has dark bluish-gray plumage (covering of feathers) with lighter underparts. Its tail is gray in the center and has white edges. The female is reddish-brown in color with lighter underparts. It has a brown tail with black and pale yellow edges.

An average purple-winged ground-dove measures 9 inches (23 centimeters) in length. Bamboo seeds make up the bulk of the bird's diet. It also feeds on fruit, grass seeds, and sedges (grassy plants growing in wet areas).

The purple-winged ground-dove is quite rare. When seen, it is usually in a small flock. Not much is known about the bird's breeding habits

The purple-winged ground-dove is native to Argentina, Brazil, and Paraguay. © LUIZ CLAUDIO MARIGO/NATUREPL .COM.

other than the fact that its breeding season begins in November or December when bamboo plants begin to flower.

Habitat and current distribution

This species is found only in the Atlantic forest region of southeastern South America. Although there are occasional sightings at various locations throughout its range, the bird is considered very rare. As of the 2010s, scientists estimate there are 70 to 400 individuals in the wild.

Purple-winged ground-doves prefer to inhabit dense forests and forest borders with nearby bamboo plants. They tend to build their nests in thick, bushy trees.

History and conservation measures

Because the purple-winged ground-dove is such a specialized eater (mainly bamboo seeds), it requires a large range in which to find the necessary amount of food. Even moderate deforestation (large-scale removal of trees) greatly reduces the bird's habitat and food source and may already have increased the possibility of the species' extinction.

The purple-winged ground-dove is legally protected throughout its range. A complete ban on capturing wild specimens has been recommended. It is thought to exist in small numbers in some parks and reserves along the Serra do Mar, a mountain range in southern Brazil, and at the Iguazú National Park in Argentina. Since little is known about the purple-winged ground-dove's particular needs, however, no special measures have been taken on its behalf in those parks. Protection of the particular species of bamboo on which it feeds would be helpful, according to conservationists (people who work to manage and protect nature).

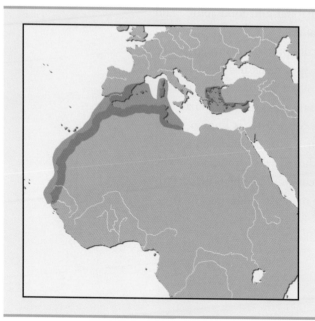

Gull, Audouin's
Larus audouinii

PHYLUM: Chordata
CLASS: Aves
ORDER: Charadriiformes
FAMILY: Laridae
STATUS: Near threatened, IUCN
Endangered, ESA
RANGE: Algeria, Croatia, Cyprus,
France, Gambia, Gibraltar, Greece, Italy,
Libya, Mauritania, Morocco, Portugal,
Senegal, Spain, Tunisia, Turkey

Gull, Audouin's
Larus audouinii

Description and biology

Gulls are aquatic birds found near all oceans and many inland waters around the world. Audouin's gull is a moderately large gull, with a length ranging from 19 to 20.5 inches (48 to 52 centimeters). Its plumage (covering of feathers) is pale gray and white. It has black wing tips and a black-and-red bill. The bird feeds primarily on fish it plucks from the sea while in flight.

The breeding season for Audouin's gulls lasts from April until June. The female lays two or three eggs in a depression she has scraped out in the ground. Both parents incubate (sit on or brood) the eggs for about 28 days until they hatch. The young gulls are fed and raised by both parents. They fledge (develop flying feathers) after about 35 to 40 days and become completely independent after three or four months.

The Audouin's gull is native to southern Europe and northern Africa. © TXANBELIN/SHUTTERSTOCK.COM.

Habitat and current distribution

Audouin's gulls breed primarily in the western Mediterranean, on rocky islets (very small islands) far from human civilization. The main breeding areas of Audouin's gulls are in northeastern Spain and in the Chafarinas Islands off the coast of Morocco. There are also scattered colonies as far west as Portugal and as far east as the Aegean Sea. These gulls usually feed over water not far from land. They nest on small, low-lying islands covered with grass or low bushes.

Biologists (people who study living organisms) have estimated the total population of the species as it has improved over the years, from about 800 to 900 male-female pairs in 1965 to 15,000 pairs in 1995 to 19,200 pairs in 2000. As of 2015, biologists estimated that there were between 43,000 and 44,000 mature Audouin's gulls in Europe alone. The population is in fact larger than this after taking into account younger birds and the Audouin's gulls in Africa, which are assumed to make up 5 percent of the total global population.

History and conservation measures

European programs to preserve the Audouin's gull began in the early to mid-1990s. At that time, scientists feared that the species' population would start to decrease quickly. The bird has been the focus of much research. Data collected show that the species' population did not decrease in the early 21st century. In fact, there may in fact be more Audouin's gulls in Europe than ever before.

The significant increase in the population of Audouin's gulls is largely the result of an increase in the fish it eats in the western Mediterranean. Despite its remarkable rise in numbers, the species remains vulnerable. The primary threat facing Audouin's gulls is having their breeding areas disturbed by people, especially fishers, tourists, and shepherds. Because some of these areas are unprotected, many people collect the birds' eggs. The gulls are also threatened by pollution, which is destroying their feeding areas.

Hawk, Galápagos
Buteo galapagoensis

PHYLUM: Chordata
CLASS: Aves
ORDER: Accipitriformes
FAMILY: Accipitridae
STATUS: Vulnerable, IUCN
Endangered, ESA
RANGE: Ecuador (Galápagos Islands)

Hawk, Galápagos
Buteo galapagoensis

Description and biology

Hawks are members of the family that includes eagles, kites, and Old World vultures—all birds of prey. The Galápagos hawk is deep dark brown with lighter markings on its sides and belly. It has a gray tail with dark bars and a yellow, dark-tipped bill. An average adult measures 21 to 23 inches (53 to 58 centimeters) long.

While young sea iguanas form the bulk of its diet, this bird will also eat a variety of other birds, rats, and lizards. It also feeds on carrion (the decaying flesh of dead animals). While flying, the hawk soars to great heights, then swoops down on prey in a zigzag pattern.

Galápagos hawks generally form groups that stake out or claim territory within their habitat. These groups typically consist of two to three males and one female, although some groups have been known to include up to eight males. They breed all year but more frequently between May and July. Females usually lay one to three eggs. After hatching, all of the males in the group help with raising the young chicks.

Habitat and current distribution

The Galápagos hawk is found only on the Galápagos Islands of Santiago, Isabela, Pinta, Santa Fe, Española, Fernandina, Marchena, and Pinzón. A province of Ecuador, the Galápagos Islands lie about 600 miles (966 kilometers) off the west coast of the country. Biologists (people who study living organisms) estimate that there were 400 to 500 adult Galápagos hawks and 300 to 400 young in existence as of 2007.

The species lives in all Galápagos habitats, including coasts, lava fields, rocky scrub (land covered with stunted trees and shrubs) and brush areas, forests, and mountains. The hawks prefer to nest in low

The Galápagos hawk was found on most of the Galápagos Islands until about the 1930s. © WATCHTHEWORLD/SHUTTERSTOCK.COM.

trees or on rocky outcrops. Much of their range lies within Galápagos National Park, which covers all areas of the islands that are uninhabited by humans.

History and conservation measures

Until the 1930s the Galápagos hawk was found on almost all of the Galápagos Islands. It existed in such great numbers that it was considered a threat to domestic chickens. Eventually, though, the number of Galápagos hawks began to decline. This was the direct result of hunting by humans and the destruction of its habitat. Human threats are now uncommon but can still be a problem on the inhabited islands of Santa Cruz and Isabela. Other threats to the species include competition for food with other predators and feral (once domesticated, now wild) cats, as well as low genetic diversity (variety of biological units that pass on inherited traits), which results when the population is small and individuals mate with relatives. Low genetic diversity can make the hawks less healthy and more prone to getting diseases and parasites (organisms that live on and feed on another species) such as lice.

The hawk is now considered extinct on the Galápagos Islands of Baltra, Daphne, Floreana, San Cristóbal, and Seymour. Ecuadorian law has protected the Galápagos hawk since 1959. Scientists have studied the possibility of introducing the species to other Galápagos Islands. However, they believe that the hawks may not have enough animals to hunt and eat in other islands, and that their presence could harm other endangered species on those islands.

Hawk, Hawaiian
Buteo solitarius

PHYLUM: Chordata
CLASS: Aves
ORDER: Accipitriformes
FAMILY: Accipitridae
STATUS: Near threatened, IUCN
Endangered, ESA
RANGE: USA (Hawaii)

Hawk, Hawaiian
Buteo solitarius

Description and biology

The Hawaiian hawk, called the *'io* in Hawaiian, is the only broad-winged hawk native to the Hawaiian Islands. Its plumage (covering of feathers) varies from dark brown to tawny brown to almost white. Dark spots mark its chest and belly and the undersides of its wings. An average adult Hawaiian hawk measures 16 to 18 inches (41 to 46 centimeters) long. Females are slightly larger than males.

The Hawaiian hawk is an agile flier, performing acrobatic movements at great heights. It often soars on the thermals, or warm air currents, above volcanoes. The bird generally hunts from a perch in a tree, swooping down on its prey. Its diet is composed of insects and small birds, although it now hunts the game birds and rodents that human settlers have introduced to its island habitat.

A male-female pair builds a nest fairly low in a tree and then reuses it each year, adding sticks and branches. Nesting begins in March, with the female laying a single egg in April or May. She broods, or sits on the egg, for 38 days, while the male hunts and brings home food. The young hawk fledges (develops flying feathers) after seven or eight weeks but remains dependent on its parents for up to nine months. The Hawaiian hawk has one of the longest parental care periods of the *Buteo* genus (a group with similar characteristics). Its slow reproductive rate may make it more difficult for the species to maintain stable populations in a changing habitat.

Habitat and current distribution

The Hawaiian hawk breeds on the island of Hawaii (also known as the Big Island) but ranges as far as the islands of Maui and Oahu. It is found from sea level to 8,500 feet (2,590 meters) of altitude but generally prefers elevations below 5,500 feet (1,675 meters). The bird has adapted to various habitats, including light woodland, forests, and farmland or other cultivated areas bordered by trees. Although it can nest in a broad range of habitat, it prefers native *'ōhi'a lehua* trees, whose numbers are generally in decline.

Biologists (people who study living organisms) estimate the Hawaiian hawk population to be about 3,000.

History and conservation measures

The largest threat to this species is the clearing of the native forest for agricultural, industrial, and residential use. Although Hawaiian hawks are known to adapt to a changed habitat, they typically prefer native forest. The hawks are also threatened by human encounters, including being shot, being hit by vehicles, and being poisoned, as well as being preyed on by introduced species, including dogs, cats, and mongooses.

The Hawaiian hawk has been legally protected by the United States since 1967, when it was placed on the Endangered Species List. Recovery efforts—including forest restoration, habitat monitoring, and control of introduced species—have allowed the species population to grow from a few hundred individuals to almost 3,000. An island-wide survey of the hawks carried out in 2007 allowed for the further development of a species-monitoring program.

Although the Hawaiian hawk is still listed as endangered under the Endangered Species Act, proposals to reclassify it as threatened or to

The Hawaiian hawk, which lives in several types of habitats, is vulnerable to agricultural and residential development that can disturb its nesting grounds. © DESIGN PICS INC/ALAMY.

delist it entirely have been made since 1993. The original documents for delisting were submitted by an organization partly founded to repeal the Endangered Species Act, but the proposal has been considered now that the hawk appears to be at least partially recovered. Many Hawaiians, however, want to keep the hawk on the Endangered Species List because of the animal's importance to native culture. The Hawaiian hawk is considered *ʻaumakua*—that is, a family god in the form of an animal—to many native Hawaiians.

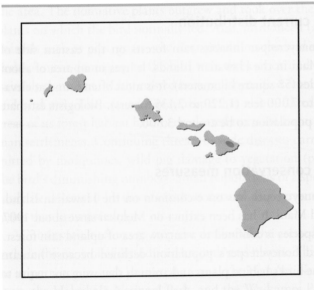

Honeycreeper, crested
Palmeria dolei

PHYLUM: Chordata
CLASS: Aves
ORDER: Passeriformes
FAMILY: Fringillidae
STATUS: Critically endangered, IUCN
Endangered, ESA
RANGE: USA (Hawaii)

Honeycreeper, crested
Palmeria dolei

Description and biology

The crested honeycreeper, called the *'akohekohe* in Hawaiian, is a song-bird. An adult of the species has an average length of 7 inches (18 centimeters). Its black plumage (covering of feathers) is speckled with gray and orange. It has orange bars on its wings and an orange band on the back of its neck. The bird's bill is straight and pointed, and it has a grayish-white tuft on its forehead.

The crested honeycreeper feeds on nectar from the flowers of the *'ōhi'a lehua* tree (a tree with bright red flowers and hard wood that is in the myrtle family). It also feeds on nectar from a number of other flowering plants. In addition, the bird eats insects and fruits.

Biologists (people who study living organisms) know little about the crested honeycreeper's reproductive habits. They believe the bird begins to build a nest in February or March. A female crested honeycreeper will generally lay one or two eggs shortly afterward, but it is not known how long it takes the eggs to hatch.

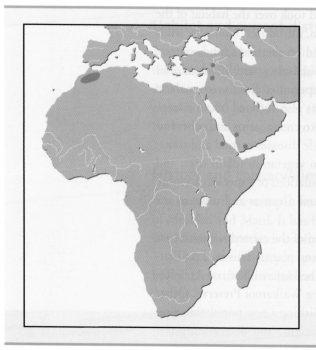

Ibis, northern bald
Geronticus eremita

PHYLUM: Chordata
CLASS: Aves
ORDER: Pelecaniformes
FAMILY: Threskiornithidae
STATUS: Critically endangered, IUCN
Endangered, ESA
RANGE: Algeria, Eritrea, Jordan, Morocco, Saudi Arabia, Syria, Turkey, Yemen

Ibis, northern bald

Geronticus eremita

Description and biology

The northern bald ibis, also known as the waldrapp, grows to an average length of 27.5 to 31.5 inches (70 to 80 centimeters). The bird's naked red head and fringe of dark feathers around its neck give it the appearance of a vulture. Its feathers, chiefly black in color, have an iridescent bronze-green gloss. A patch on its forewing or "shoulder" is a shade of shiny bronze-purple. The northern bald ibis has a long tapering bill that curves downward. It uses its bill to probe for and feed on insects, such as beetles and grasshoppers, and fish and other aquatic animals.

The northern bald ibis nests in colonies of up to 40 pairs of birds, usually on rocky cliffs or ledges in semiarid and arid (partly dry and dry) areas near water. The breeding season begins in February. In late March or early April, after making a nest of straw, grasses, and twigs, a female

The northern bald ibis is a migratory bird whose feathers have an iridescent bronze-green gloss. © BELIZAR/SHUTTERSTOCK.COM.

northern bald ibis lays a clutch (number of eggs produced at one time) of three to four eggs. In about 60 days, the nestlings will have hatched and fledged (developed flying feathers). By the end of June, they will leave the nesting grounds with their parents.

Main predators of the bald ibis include ravens (which sometimes prey on nestlings or eggs) and falcons (which have been seen attacking nesting ibises).

Habitat and current distribution

The northern bald ibis is considered critically endangered. The majority of these birds can be found in Morocco in northwest Africa. Biologists

The Mauritius kestrel population has been negatively affected by loss of habitat, pesticide use, nonnative plants, and inbreeding on its island home.
© RGB VENTURES/SUPERSTOCK/ ALAMY.

take 30 to 32 days to hatch. After hatching, the young kestrels may stay with their parents until the beginning of the next breeding season.

Habitat and current distribution

The Mauritius kestrel is confined to remote areas in the southwestern part of Mauritius Island, which lies in the Indian Ocean about 450 miles (724 kilometers) east of the island of Madagascar. The bird prefers to inhabit cool evergreen forests where the trees form a canopy (uppermost layer of a forest) about 50 feet (15 meters) above the ground.

Biologists (people who study living organisms) estimated the bird's population as of 2012 at 400 kestrels, including 250 to 300 birds old enough to reproduce.

History and conservation measures

When Mauritius was covered in vast forests, the kestrel was found throughout the island. Heavy logging and clearing of the forests in the 20th century destroyed the Mauritius kestrel's habitat and food sources. By the 1950s, the bird was found only in the remote forests of the southwestern plateau. Population declines continued as a result of heavy pesticide use in the species' range in the 1950s and 1960s. By 1974 only four birds were estimated to remain in the wild. In such a small population, inbreeding (animals mating with relatives) cannot be avoided, since offspring all trace their ancestry to the same group of parents. This results in a significant loss of genetic diversity (variety of biological units that pass on inherited traits) and offspring are more likely to suffer from genetic diseases.

Conservation efforts have focused on preserving the habitat of the Mauritius kestrel. In 1974 the 8,880-acre (3,552-hectare) Macabé–Bel Ombre Nature Reserve was created. In 1994 Black River Gorges National Park was established, linking the nature reserve with other areas and providing a greater protected region.

Conservation programs in Mauritius monitored the birds in the wild, cared for rescued eggs, and bred the birds in captivity to release into the wild. Food was provided for the kestrels, and they were provided with nest boxes to help protect their nests from introduced predators, such as rats, monkeys, and mongooses.

A successful captive-breeding program introduced 346 kestrels back into the wild by 1994. At the end of that decade, the population was estimated at up to 800 kestrels. However, some of the new kestrel populations did not survive due to further loss of their natural habitat. By 2012 the population had declined to about 400 kestrels. This decline led the International Union for Conservation of Nature and Natural Resources (IUCN) to uplist (change to a worsened status) the Mauritius kestrel from vulnerable to endangered in 2014. However, scientists believe that the species still has a good chance for survival. The kestrels' population and their breeding activities continue to be monitored.

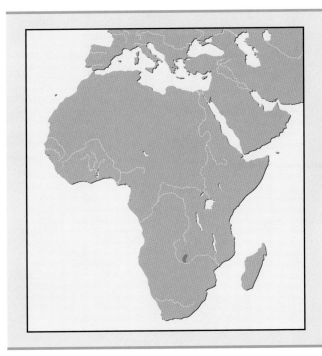

Lovebird, black-cheeked
Agapornis nigrigenis

PHYLUM: Chordata
CLASS: Aves
ORDER: Psittaciformes
FAMILY: Psittacidae
STATUS: Vulnerable, IUCN
RANGE: Zambia

Lovebird, black-cheeked
Agapornis nigrigenis

Description and biology

Lovebirds are small African parrots that measure about 5.5 inches (14 centimeters) long. The black-cheeked lovebird is perhaps the most threatened of all lovebird species in the wild. This bird is primarily green, with a dark brown head and a white eye-ring. Its forehead is reddish brown. It feeds mainly on seeds, grass seeds, and leaves. Access to water is important for these birds, which have to drink twice a day. In the dry season, when the birds are not breeding, they are known to flock in groups of up to 800 birds near watering sites.

Breeding takes place from January to May during the end of the rainy season and the beginning of the dry season. Male-female pairs remain together and use the same nest site year after year. Nests are made in natural holes in the mopane tree, where the female lays a clutch (number of eggs produced at one time) of six to seven eggs.

The black-cheeked lovebird was the target of pet traders in the early 20th century, but loss of habitat is what now threatens the species in its native Zambia. © BLICKWINKEL/ALAMY.

Habitat and current distribution

The black-cheeked lovebird is confined mainly to the extreme southwestern part of Zambia. It is possible that the bird can be found also in Botswana, Zimbabwe, and Namibia, but scientists have not been able to confirm the sightings in those countries. The total number of black-cheeked lovebirds currently in existence is unknown. In 2013 it was estimated that there might be as few as 3,500 birds in the wild.

The bird prefers to inhabit medium-altitude forests dominated by deciduous trees (trees whose leaves fall off annually), where there is also access to water. The total habitat range is about 5,560 square miles (14,400 square kilometers).

History and conservation measures

In the 20th century, black-cheeked lovebirds were trapped and sold around the world as caged pets. During a four-week period in 1929, as many as 16,000 of the birds were captured. The species has never recovered from this assault.

Despite legal protection in Zambia, this lovebird is still sometimes trapped illegally, although very few birds are caught in the wild anymore. It remains a common cage bird, however. Lovebirds sold as pets come from breeders who mate the birds in captivity.

In the wild, black-cheeked lovebirds continue to be threatened by the draining of water sources from their habitat in order to supply agricultural needs. The bird's habitat area is also drying out due to decreased rainfall in southwestern Zambia, a condition that some scientists believe could be linked to global climate change. The destruction of its habitat to create farmland also remains a potential threat.

Macaw, Lear's
Anodorhynchus leari

PHYLUM: Chordata
CLASS: Aves
ORDER: Psittaciformes
FAMILY: Psittacidae
STATUS: Endangered, IUCN
Endangered, ESA
RANGE: Brazil

Macaw, Lear's
Anodorhynchus leari

Description and biology

Macaws are members of the parrot family. Lear's macaw is also known as the indigo macaw because the color of its plumage (covering of feathers) is a beautiful indigo, or dark purplish blue. It has grayish-green accents on its head and breast. A yellow patch appears at the base of the bird's black bill. Its legs are dark gray. An average Lear's macaw measures 30 inches (76 centimeters) long. Its average life span is about 40 years.

This bird uses its bill as well as its feet for climbing. Its preferred food is the small nut that grows on the licuri palm tree. Each day before sunrise, the flock of Lear's macaws is awakened by the loud cawing of individual "scout" macaws. The flock then leaves its nesting area for its feeding grounds.

Lear's macaw has been the focus of conservation efforts that have increased the bird's population in its native Brazil. Here, two Lear's macaws feed on palm nuts. © PETE OXFORD/MINDEN PICTURES/CORBIS.

Lear's macaws mate between February and April and produce an average of two young.

Habitat and current distribution

Lear's macaw lives in the northern part of the northeastern Brazilian state of Bahia. It prefers to inhabit deep canyons and desertlike plateaus, sleeping and nesting in burrowed tunnels in sandstone cliffs. In 2014 biologists (people who study living organisms) estimated the population of Lear's macaws to be around 1,300.

History and conservation measures

Lear's macaw is probably one of the rarest parrots in the world. Only captive-bred birds were known until 1979, when biologists discovered a wild population in a remote area of Brazil. In the early 1990s the population in the wild was only about 65 birds.

Damage to the licuri palm tree, and the hard nutlike seeds that are the bird's main food source, has posed the major threat to Lear's macaw. Farmers burn down palms to clear land for agriculture, goats eat the trees, and cattle trample the trees' roots. Another major threat has been the illegal capturing of the birds for the international pet trade.

Conservationists (people who work to manage and protect nature) have worked hard to save Lear's macaw from extinction. Nonprofit groups have bought and are protecting the land where almost 75 percent of the birds live. They have reduced illegal trapping and smuggling of the birds. More licuri palms are being planted, and people are monitoring the birds and educating local people about their importance. In 2009, based on the success of these efforts, the International Union for Conservation of Nature and Natural Resources (IUCN) downlisted the bird's status from critically endangered to endangered.

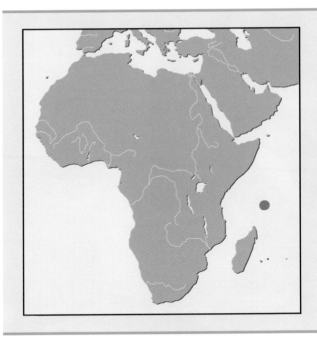

Magpie-robin, Seychelles
Copsychus sechellarum

PHYLUM: Chordata
CLASS: Aves
ORDER: Passeriformes
FAMILY: Muscicapidae
STATUS: Endangered, IUCN
Endangered, ESA
RANGE: Seychelles

Magpie-robin, Seychelles
Copsychus sechellarum

Description and biology

The Seychelles magpie-robin is a thrushlike bird with fairly long legs. Adult birds are between 7.1 and 8.3 inches (18 and 21 centimeters) long. The color of its plumage (covering of feathers) is glossy black. Large white patches appear on each wing. The bird's diet includes small lizards and a small amount of fruit.

A female Seychelles magpie-robin lays one egg per year. She incubates (sits on or broods) the egg for 16 to 20 days. After the nestling hatches, it remains in the nest for about three weeks. It becomes independent after another three to five weeks.

Habitat and current distribution

This bird species now survives only on the islands of Frégate, Cousin, Cousine, Aride, and Denis, which are part of the Seychelles, an island

The Seychelles magpie-robin has responded to conservation efforts beginning in the 1990s to increase its population in its native island habitat. © WIL MEINDERTS/BUITEN-BEELD/MINDEN PICTURES/CORBIS.

republic located in the Indian Ocean, lying east of the African country of Tanzania. Biologists (people who study living organisms) estimated that in 2009, about 200 birds existed in the wild on the five islands.

Historically, the Seychelles magpie-robin inhabited coastal forests. However, that habitat was cleared to create farmland. In response, the bird has adapted to living on plantations that grow cashews, citrus trees, coconut trees, or coffee. It can also be found in vegetable gardens. The bird normally nests in tree holes.

History and conservation measures

Now one of the rarest birds in the world, the magpie-robin was once a very common bird in the Seychelles Islands group. It disappeared quite early in the 20th century from several of the islands. The bird was present on the islands of Marianne and Aride until the 1930s and on Alphonse until the late 1950s. By 1959 only 10 pairs were known to survive on Frégate Island.

The Seychelles Magpie-Robin Recovery Program was started by BirdLife International in 1990. Birds were relocated to other islands and, within a few years, the Seychelles magpie-robin population had doubled. The population has continued to rise since then, and as a result, the International Union for Conservation of Nature and Natural Resources (IUCN) changed the status of the species from critically endangered to endangered in 2005.

Although this bird has been able to adapt to the loss of its habitat, it has not fared well against predators brought to the islands by humans. A tame, ground-feeding bird, it has been an easy prey for rats and feral (once domesticated, now wild) cats. In the 1960s efforts were made to control the feral cat population. By 1982 most feral cats had been eliminated from Frégate, and rats were eliminated by 2000. The bird relocations focused on islands that were free of predators.

The Seychelles magpie-robin also faces competition for nesting sites and food sources from the Indian myna, a bird that was introduced to the Seychelles Islands in the early 1800s. However, nest boxes provided by the recovery program protect the nests of the Seychelles magpie-robin. Another threat to these birds are household pesticides. The Seychelles magpie-robin eats cockroaches, dead or alive, and in the past, poisons from household pesticides used to kill cockroaches also harmed the birds. Since biologists became aware of that danger, pesticide use has been banned or restricted, and alternative bird-safe pesticides have been researched and permitted.

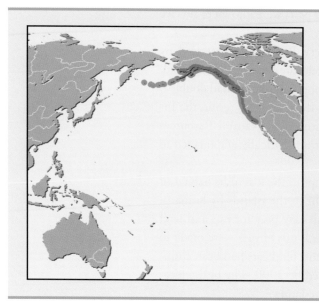

Murrelet, marbled
Brachyramphus marmoratus

PHYLUM: Chordata
CLASS: Aves
ORDER: Charadriiformes
FAMILY: Alcidae
STATUS: Endangered, IUCN
Threatened, ESA (in California, Oregon, and Washington)
RANGE: Canada, USA (Alaska, California, Oregon, Washington)

Murrelet, marbled
Brachyramphus marmoratus

Description and biology

The marbled murrelet (pronounced MURR-let) belongs to the family of diving seabirds known as auks, or alcids, which includes species such as puffins, murres, auklets, and guillemots (pronounced GI-luh-mahts). The marbled murrelet is small and chunky, with a wingspan of 9.5 to 10 inches (24 to 25 centimeters). It weighs about 10.6 ounces (300 grams). It has webbed feet, a sharp black bill, and pointed wings. Like many other birds, the murrelet grows two sets of feathers each year. In summer, its plumage (covering of feathers) is marbled in shades of dark brown and light gray. In winter, its upperparts are black while its underparts are white.

Murrelets generally feed within 2 miles (3.2 kilometers) of shore. They prey on small fish, such as sand lances, capelins, herring, and smelt. They pursue their prey underwater, diving well below the surface. Steering with their webbed feet, they use their wings like flippers to pro-

The marbled murrelet, native to the United States and Canada, has seen its nesting grounds disturbed by logging activity, which has caused a large drop in its population. © TIM ZUROWSKI/ALL CANADA PHOTOS/CORBIS.

pel themselves forward. Often, a dive will last no more than 30 seconds. Predators of the murrelet include peregrine falcons and bald eagles.

Marbled murrelets nest primarily in old-growth forests (forests that have developed over a long period) where the trees range from 175 to 600 years old. Although most nesting sites are located within 12 miles (19.5 kilometers) of shore, some have been found up to 50 miles (80 kilometers) away from the ocean. The birds build their nests on natural platforms underneath an overhanging branch, often at a height of more than 100 feet (30 meters) above the ground.

Breeding season lasts from mid-April to the end of August. After a male and female marbled murrelet mate, the female lays one large, spotted, yellowish egg. Both the male and the female incubate (sit on or brood) the egg, and incubation lasts for about 30 days. After hatching, the nestling, or young bird, stays in the nest for about another 28 days before it fledges (develops flying feathers).

Habitat and current distribution

Marbled murrelets are found near coastal waters, bays, and mountains from Alaska's Aleutian Islands and Kenai Peninsula south along the coast of North America to Santa Barbara County in south-central California. In winter, they leave the northernmost parts of their range and travel as far south as San Diego County, California.

A 2012 study estimated the total population of murrelets at between 350,000 and 420,000 individuals. The majority of murrelets breed along the Alaskan coast. Murrelet populations are much smaller in the southern part of their range, along the coasts of California, Oregon, and Washington, where their total population was estimated at about 19,600 as of 2013.

History and conservation measures

Because marbled murrelets face few natural threats in their environment, they can live as long as 25 years. However, human activities can have a serious effect on the birds. Oil pollution, fishing nets, and habitat loss have all combined to threaten the existence of this bird. The U.S. Fish and Wildlife Service lists the species as threatened in California, Oregon, and Washington. The marbled murrelet remains abundant in Alaska, but it is listed as endangered across its entire range by the International Union for Conservation of Nature and Natural Resources (IUCN) because of the rapid decline in its population.

The greatest threat to the marbled murrelet is the loss of its habitat stemming from the clear-cutting (the process of cutting down all the trees) of old-growth forests. Since the early 20th century, much of the old-growth forests along the Pacific coast have been cleared. Very little of the existing old-growth forest is currently protected.

Concern has also been raised about the number of murrelets killed in gill nets, which are fishing nets designed to catch fish by their gills and drown them. These nets, however, end up catching many different aquatic creatures, including murrelets. Studies have reported that 600 to 800 or more marbled murrelets are killed annually in gill nets in Prince William Sound, Alaska, alone.

Because the marbled murrelet feeds close to shore, it is highly vulnerable to oil spills and other types of water pollution. The development of the petroleum industry along the Pacific coast has increased the threat of oil pollution in the murrelet's range. Reports in the early 21st century showed that the murrelet had also been harmed by the collapse of the Pacific sardine fishery and had to rely on a diet of krill, small shrimplike crustaceans (shellfish). This change in diet is believed to have resulted in a decline in the number of murrelets reaching breeding age.

The marbled murrelet's range has been protected in both Canada and the United States. For example, in British Columbia, about 35 percent of suitable murrelet habitat was protected by 2011. Conservationists (people who work to manage and protect nature) believe that additional research on nesting habits would also help the murrelet and that protection of old-growth forests is essential to their survival.

A 1999 study also suggested that the murrelet would be helped by moving human campgrounds away from old-growth forests. The campgrounds attract crows, ravens, and related birds that scavenge garbage but also prey on murrelet eggs. Such predators are thought to be one of the main reasons for the decline in the California marbled murrelet population in the first decade of the 21st century.

The northern spotted owl, native to North America, lives almost exclusively in old-growth forests dominated by Douglas fir, western hemlock, and redwood trees. © ALL CANADA PHOTOS/ALAMY.

Lumber companies argued that preserving old-growth forests would cost jobs and hurt the economy, while environmentalists stated that the lumber companies were simply delaying what was destined to happen: at the rate lumber companies were cutting trees, the old-growth forests would soon disappear, and just as many people would become unemployed. In addition, conservationists (people who work to manage and protect nature) contended that old-growth forests are necessary for the survival of many species, not only the northern spotted owl but also the marbled murrelet and the red-cockaded woodpecker, among others.

In 1993, at the request of U.S. president Bill Clinton, a team of specialists, including scientists and economists, began a study of how best to manage the federally owned forests of the Pacific Northwest and Northern California. That study was used in creating the Northwest Forest Plan, which was adopted by the Clinton administration in 1994. The plan contained a series of federal policies and guidelines governing forest use in the region. The federal government and the lumber companies hoped this was the beginning of a solution to save both jobs and the northern spotted owl and other species.

In the 21st century scientists have identified competition from the barred owl for food and territory space as a significant cause for the continued reduction of northern spotted owl populations. The U.S. Fish and Wildlife Service has been investigating whether removing barred owls from the forests would give the northern spotted owl a chance to increase its numbers. Research into whether this strategy would be effective began in 2013 and involves removal of 3,600 barred owls from 2 percent of spotted owl habitat to determine how the spotted owl population is affected.

The International Union for Conservation of Nature and Natural Resources (IUCN) lists the spotted owl (*Strix occidentalis*), including the northern spotted owl and the other three subspecies, as near threatened because of its relatively small population and the continuing decline of the species.

In the 1990s it was thought that the population had been reduced to 2,500 individuals, but that estimate has turned out to be low. Scientists in 2011 estimated that there were between 10,000 and 20,000 golden parakeets in Brazil, but their numbers are thought to be decreasing.

History and conservation measures

Scientists have long considered the golden parakeet rare. Where good forest remains, the bird may still be seen regularly. Nonetheless, the overall number of golden parakeets has declined sharply.

Habitat destruction is the primary threat to the golden parakeet. Widespread clearing of the tropical forest to build roads and settlements has destroyed much of the bird's habitat in Maranhão. Major development projects, such as railroad construction, logging, cattle ranching, and gold mining, have also contributed to the decline of its habitat. However, the birds are less reliant on extensive forests than was once thought and can move across non-wooded areas to other fragments of their habitat. The destruction of their forest habitats is also less extensive than earlier researchers assumed.

Golden parakeets used to be seriously threatened by hunting; they were among the most highly prized birds in the world and smuggling was frequent. Increased protections have reduced illegal captures. In addition, there are now enough captive birds to satisfy most of the demand by collectors. This has reduced the demand for smuggling wild specimens.

Because hunting has decreased, and because of the bird's surprising adaptability, the status of the golden parakeet was changed by the International Union for Conservation of Nature and Natural Resources (IUCN) from endangered to vulnerable in 2013. Still, habitat destruction continues, and scientists predicted that the bird's numbers, from that 2013 starting point, would drop dangerously over the three generations to follow.

The only well-protected nature reserve in the golden parakeet's western range is the Tapajós (Amazonia) National Park in Pará. Conservationists (people who work to manage and protect nature) believe that additional areas in its range must be protected and managed so the golden parakeet can survive and breed. They also have called for more captive-breeding programs and more legal restrictions on trade.

Parrot, imperial
Amazona imperialis

PHYLUM: Chordata
CLASS: Aves
ORDER: Psittaciformes
FAMILY: Psittacidae
STATUS: Endangered, IUCN
Endangered, ESA
RANGE: Dominica

Parrot, imperial
Amazona imperialis

Description and biology

The imperial parrot, known as the sisserou in the Caribbean republic of Dominica, is a large parrot. An average adult measures 18 to 20 inches (46 to 51 centimeters) in length and weighs about 2 pounds (0.9 kilograms). It has a wingspan of about 30 inches (76 centimeters). The color of the bird's plumage (covering of feathers) on its upper parts and back is green. Its head is greenish blue, and it has a red streak on its wingtips. The bird feeds primarily on seeds, fruit, young shoots, vines, and shrubs.

Parrots mate for life. The imperial parrot's breeding season lasts from February to June, with peak breeding taking place between March and May. Male and female pairs rarely leave their nesting territory throughout the year. On average, a female imperial parrot lays two eggs every

The imperial parrot, native to the Caribbean island of Dominica, was threatened by habitat loss and pet traders until conservation programs were enacted in the 1990s to protect and increase its population. © PETRA WEGNER/ALAMY.

Did You Know?

Aviculture (pronounced A-vi-kul-chur) is the keeping and raising of birds—especially wild birds—in captivity. Humans have kept songbirds, such as canaries, and other caged birds for thousands of years. It was not until the mid-20th century, however, that bird keepers learned to successfully breed parrots and other exotic wild birds in captivity. As a result, the demand for parrots as caged birds increased, and large numbers were captured in the wild to meet the new demand, putting many parrot species at risk. International conservation organizations soon opposed the capture of wild parrots, and concerned nations enacted laws against the capture and trade of wild birds.

However, despite international prohibitions, the illegal trade in birds, especially parrots, is bustling. In Latin America alone, biologists (people who study living organisms) estimate that between 400,000 and 800,000 parrot chicks are taken from their nests each year. Many of the captured birds die before they reach a purchaser. As birds become more endangered, their rarity makes them more valuable to poachers (illegal hunters), who can fetch a higher price for them.

A hope for parrots and other illegally traded animals is to promote ecotourism, which brings tourists to pristine natural habitats to view wildlife. Such tourism brings income to communities near these natural areas, and it gives the local people a reason to protect, rather than hunt or collect, the endangered species that live there. However, such tourism also increases the human presence near natural habitats, which itself can disturb threatened species.

other year in a nest high in the trunk of a tree. It is unknown how long it takes the eggs to hatch. After the eggs do hatch, usually only one of the nestlings survives to adulthood.

Habitat and current distribution

The imperial parrot is unique to the island of Dominica, which lies in the center of the Lesser Antilles between Guadeloupe and Martinique. It is Dominica's national bird, and its image appears at the center of the republic's flag.

The imperial parrot is primarily found in and around the forests of the two highest mountains in Dominica: Morne Diablotin in the northern part of the island and, in smaller numbers, Morne Trois Pitons at the southern end of the island. The parrot is found chiefly at elevations between 1,969 and 4,265 feet (600 and 1,300 meters). In search for food, the imperial parrot goes to much lower elevations, down to 492 feet (150 meters). Biologists (people who study living organisms) estimate that 250 to 350 imperial parrots existed in the wild as of 2012.

History and conservation measures

In the past, the imperial parrot was probably found throughout the mountainous island of Dominica, although the center of its range has most likely always been Morne Diablotin.

Early threats to the parrot included humans hunting it for food, for sport, and for the pet trade. In the 1880s a road was built through the bird's forest habitat, allowing hunters easy access to the area, further endangering the imperial parrot. These conditions did not improve until Hurricane David struck Dominica in 1979 and destroyed millions of trees. Following this disaster, officials imposed a ban on the hunting of all wildlife and forest patrols have since kept most hunters at bay. Because of laws that protect the imperial parrot, as well as increased awareness and pride among the local people about the bird, poaching (illegal hunting) has not been a significant threat since the 1990s.

Because of the bird's remote range, habitat destruction was not considered a threat to the parrot until the late 20th century. Beginning in the 1980s prime forest land bordering the imperial parrot's habitat was cleared and converted into farmland. Conservationists (people who work to manage and protect nature) were eventually successful at designating an important portion of the imperial parrot habitat area in Dominica as a national park. The Morne Diablotin National Park now contains a significant portion of the imperial parrot habitat within its 12.9 square miles (33.4 square kilometers). However, other important habitat areas close to Dominica's forest reserves are not yet protected.

The imperial parrot is difficult to study because of its remote habitat. Its nesting and breeding habits in the wild are not well known because its nests are usually covered with vines and other plants. The first imperial parrot bred in captivity was born in 2010. Conservationists hope to develop a structured captive-breeding program for the species.

Parrot, thick-billed
Rhynchopsitta pachyrhyncha

PHYLUM: Chordata
CLASS: Aves
ORDER: Psittaciformes
FAMILY: Psittacidae
STATUS: Endangered, IUCN
Endangered, ESA
RANGE: Mexico

Parrot, thick-billed
Rhynchopsitta pachyrhyncha

Description and biology

The thick-billed parrot is about 15 inches (38 centimeters) long from head to tail. It is a bright green bird with a red forehead and red patches at the crook of the wing and thigh. Its eyes are marked with a small brownish spot and it has yellow sections under its wings and gray feathers on its lower surfaces. It has gray legs and feet and its thick bill is black.

Thick-billed parrots feed mainly on the seeds of pine trees, shredding the pinecones of a variety of conifers (evergreen trees and shrubs) in order to extract the seeds. They also eat acorns, juniper berries, flower nectar, insects, and tree bark. They hunt during the day and sleep in their roosting places high in the pine trees at night. Thick-billed parrots live in flocks, which may be as small as seven or eight members or they may be composed of a thousand or more birds. They are strong flyers, often forming a V or other formation when they fly. The birds are noted for their loud screeching calls, which can be heard from great distances.

Thick-billed parrots breed from July through September, nesting in cavities of trees at high elevations. The female lays from two to four eggs, with one or two days between each egg. While the female incubates (sits on or broods) the eggs, the male goes off in search of food during the day and brings it back to her. About 26 to 28 days later the eggs hatch, one at a time, in the order they were laid. The chicks typically have their full plumage (covering of feathers) within 56 days of birth and fly shortly thereafter. The parents remain with the chicks up to about seven months, continuing to feed them while also instructing them how to extract seeds from pinecones for themselves.

Thick-billed parrots live under constant threat from predators. When they feed, they often have one bird in the flock standing watch

The thick-billed parrot is threated by the loss of habitat in the forests of Mexico. © GEORGE H. H. HUEY/ENCYCLOPEDIA/CORBIS.

for predators, ready to signal to the other birds the moment an enemy is spotted. Their main enemies are raptors (birds of prey), such as red-tailed hawks, Apache goshawks, and peregrine falcons. When thick-billed parrots are roosting (resting or sleeping) in the trees, they are also preyed upon by ring-tailed cats.

Habitat and current distribution

Thick-billed parrots are found only in Mexico's Sierra Madre Occidental mountain range, mainly in the states of northeast Sonora, west Chihuahua, south and west Durango, and Michoacán. The birds live at elevations between 3,940 and 11,800 feet (1,200 and 3,600 meters) with nesting sites at elevations between 6,560 and 8,860 feet (2,000 and 2,700 meters).

Biologists (people who study living organisms) estimated in 2013 that there were between 2,000 and 2,800 adult thick-billed parrots in the wild. Some scientists fear the number is actually much lower, as there may be fewer than 100 active nests each year.

History and conservation measures

Thick-billed parrots once ranged from their primary habitat in northern and central Mexico as far north as southeastern Arizona and southwestern New Mexico. Early settlers in the southwest United States hunted the birds for food, virtually wiping out the entire U.S. population by the 1920s. The species continued to live in its main habitat in Mexico, but during the last decades of the 20th century, the extensive logging in the Sierra Madre Occidental mountains greatly reduced their population in Mexico. Thick-billed parrots are also captured for trade as pets.

Numerous studies are underway in an attempt to determine how to save the thick-billed parrot as its habitat continues to diminish. Because of the dangers posed by trade in the pet market, in 1975 the Convention on International Trade in Endangered Species of Wild Fauna and Flora (CITES), an international treaty to protect wildlife, listed the thick-billed parrot on its Appendix 1, which includes species threatened with extinction. This listing makes trade of the species subject to particularly strict trade regulations, authorized only under "exceptional circumstances."

A permanent research team works in the Sierra Madre Occidental to study the birds' breeding, biology, and nesting sites. In addition, Mexico has banned logging in some important thick-billed parrot habitats.

Efforts to return the thick-billed parrot to its former territory in the United States have been unsuccessful. Between 1986 and 1993, a total of 88 parrots were released in the Chiricahua Mountains in Arizona. All of the birds were quickly killed by predators or died from starvation and disease, so these efforts were suspended.

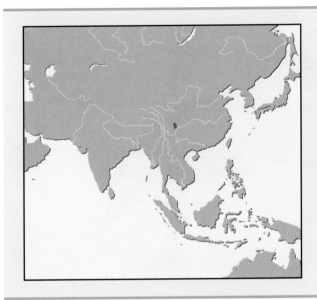

Partridge, Sichuan hill
Arborophila rufipectus

PHYLUM: Chordata
CLASS: Aves
ORDER: Galliformes
FAMILY: Phasianidae
STATUS: Endangered, IUCN
RANGE: China

Partridge, Sichuan hill
Arborophila rufipectus

Description and biology

The Sichuan hill partridge, or Sichuan partridge, is very rare and shy of humans. Little was known about the species until studies were begun in the 1990s. This partridge is about 11 inches (28 centimeters) long. It is grayish brown in color, with white markings on its forehead, a brown crown, distinctive markings around its eyes, and a black-streaked white throat. Males and females are similar in appearance except that the female coloring is not as bright.

The Sichuan hill partridge generally forages (searches for food) in the growth and litter (dead leaves and twigs) of a forest floor during the day. At night, it roosts (rests or sleeps) in high perches, except during the breeding season, when pairs roost on the ground. The species is territorial. Sichuan hill partridge male-female pairs will often send out territorial calls together. These are loud, repetitious whistles.

Sichuan hill partridges are monogamous (have just one mate for life). While the female incubates (sits on or broods) the eggs, the male

411

The main threat to the Sichuan hill partridge is destruction of its habitat, especially due to logging. © BRUCE WORDEN, MICHIGANSCIENCEART .COM.

roosts away from the nest. Biologists (people who study living organisms) believe this helps the male protect the nest from predators. After the eggs hatch, the male will join his family and help care for the chicks for about two weeks.

Habitat and current distribution

The Sichuan hill partridge is found in subtropical broadleaf cloud forests (warm, moist, forest environments that are usually under cloud cover and in which most of the trees have leaves rather than needles) at elevations of 3,600 to 7,300 feet (1,100 to 2,225 meters). The species is endemic (native to and occuring only in a particular region) to China and can be found in south-central Sichuan Province and possibly in northeastern Yunnan Province. The total population of the species was estimated to be between 1,500 and 4,000 birds as of 2012.

History and conservation measures

The primary threat to the Sichuan hill partridge is logging, which has severely reduced its habitat. The broadleaf forests in China that the bird requires for survival have been disappearing for years. By the early

1990s all of the remaining broadleaf forests inhabited by the species were scheduled to be logged. If not for the intervention of conservationists (people who work to manage and protect nature), the habitat would have been wiped out entirely. Other threats to the partridge also existed. Humans were gathering bamboo shoots, and livestock was grazing in the remaining forest areas, greatly disturbing the birds' normal behavior patterns. Since little was known about the species' habitat requirements at the time, many predicted that the partridge would be extinct by 2030.

In the mid-1990s, however, several major projects were undertaken by a variety of Chinese and international conservation groups in an effort to understand and protect the Sichuan hill partridge. The studies collected vital information about the species' distribution, population density, and habitat requirements. They revealed that altering forestry practices could benefit the partridge, especially if strips of primary forest were left along ridge tops and broadleaf trees were replanted where they had been cleared. Extensive work has continued because scientists determined that the Sichuan hill partridge serves as an excellent indicator of the ecological health of the whole region. If the species is declining, it is a clear signal of major problems throughout the ecosystem (an ecological system including all of its living things and their environment).

As it became apparent that the Sichuan hill partridge population was very low and fragmented (broken into smaller areas that no longer border each other), conservation groups put pressure on the Chinese government to alter its logging and forest management practices. The Sichuan hill partridge became a protected species within China. Other circumstances caused the Chinese government to rethink its logging practices. In 1998 catastrophic (very destructive) flooding of the Yangtze (Chang) River was linked to the logging of the slopes around it. At the same time, there were concerns about the effects that deforestation (large-scale removal of trees) was having on the Three Gorges Dam, a huge new dam on the river. In August 1998 the Chinese government enacted a ban on logging in the area, which happened to be part of the partridge's range. Since that time, local people who used to be loggers in the area have been put to work replanting the forests.

In 2001 the Sichuan Forestry Department created the first protected area for the Sichuan hill partridge at Laojunshan. The Laojunshan Nature Reserve is 91 square miles (235 square kilometers) in area and has the largest known population of Sichuan hill partridges. Two other, much larger reserves within the bird's habitat have also been established in southern Sichuan. Mamize Nature Reserve in Leibo County is 147 square miles (380 square kilometers) in area and Heizhugou Nature Reserve in Ebian Yi County is 116 square miles (300 square kilometers). Conservationists are putting new forest management practices in effect, trying to find methods that will conserve the area for the benefit of the Sichuan hill partridge as well as for other species, including humans.

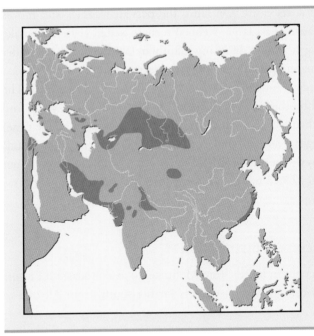

Pelican, Dalmatian
Pelecanus crispus

PHYLUM: Chordata
CLASS: Aves
ORDER: Pelecaniformes
FAMILY: Pelecanidae
STATUS: Vulnerable, IUCN
RANGE: Afghanistan, Albania, Armenia, Azerbaijan, Bangladesh, Bulgaria, China, Egypt, Georgia, Greece, India, Iran, Iraq, Israel, Kazakhstan, Kyrgyzstan, Lebanon, Moldova, Mongolia, Montenegro, Pakistan, Romania, Russia, Syria, Tajikistan, Turkey, Turkmenistan, Ukraine, Uzbekistan

Pelican, Dalmatian
Pelecanus crispus

Description and biology

The Dalmatian pelican is the largest member of the pelican family. An average adult measures 5.2 to 5.9 feet (1.6 to 1.8 meters) and weighs between 22 and 29 pounds (10 and 13 kilograms). Males are slightly larger than females. The bird has a wingspan of almost 11 feet (3.3 meters), and its long, straight bill measures between 14 and 17.5 inches (35.5 and 44.5 centimeters) in length.

This pelican has long, curly feathers on the nape of its neck. Its overall plumage (covering of feathers) is white gray in color. Dark finger-like tips mark the edges of its wings. Its legs and feet are gray black. Its pouch, which is attached to the lower part of its bill, is yellow in color most of the year. During breeding season, it turns orange red.

The Dalmatian pelican is a good flier, although it must make a heavy running start in order to take off. Once in the air, however, the bird is fast and soars easily. On land, the pelican waddles and moves awkwardly because of its large, webbed feet. In water, these feet make the bird a strong swimmer. Hunting mainly by plunging its head under water, the Dalmatian pelican feeds on a variety of fish.

Breeding season for the pelican begins in late March or April. The female, assisted by the male, builds a nest out of reed stalks, grass, and branches. She then lays a clutch (number of eggs produced at one time) of one to four eggs, and both male and female incubate (sit on or brood) them for 32 days. The nestlings fledge (develop flying feathers) about 80 days after they hatch but remain dependent on their parents for three more weeks. Crows, magpies, and gulls prey on the pelican's eggs.

Habitat and current distribution

The Dalmatian pelican breeds from Montenegro in southeastern Europe to Mongolia in central Asia; it winters farther south, from Albania to

The Dalmatian pelican, which is found across Europe and Asia, is at risk because of the decline of its wetland habitat, water pollution, hunting, and other human activity. © BELIZAR/SHUTTERSTOCK.COM.

China. The birds leave their breeding sites starting at the end of July and return between late January and April. Biologists (people who study living organisms) estimated in 2005 that the bird's total world population was between 4,350 and 4,800 in the Black Sea and the Mediterranean and between 6,000 and 9,050 in Asia.

This species of pelican prefers to inhabit estuaries (coastal waters where a freshwater river empties into a saltwater sea or ocean), lagoons, rivers, deltas, lakes, and coastal waters. Its nests are found in overgrown reeds and along seasides, lakes, deltas, and the lower reaches of rivers.

History and conservation measures

The Dalmatian pelican was once found throughout Asia and Europe, numbering in the millions. It is thought that in 1873 there were millions of pelicans in the country of Romania alone. During the 20th century the bird's population drastically declined.

Great numbers of Dalmatian pelicans have been killed by fishers, who view the birds as competitors for fish. They have also been hunted for food and for their bills, which have been used as pouches in Mongolia. Much of their habitat has been lost, as wetlands (areas where there is a lot of water in the soil, such as swamps or tidal flats) have been cleared to create farmland. Electric power lines, installed to service a growing human population throughout the bird's range, have killed many flying pelicans.

Reserves and national parks in a number of areas protect colonies of Dalmatian pelicans, including the largest Dalmatian pelican colony located at Lake Mikri Prespa in Greece. In Europe, the population of Dalmatian pelicans has increased significantly because of conservation efforts begun in the 1990s. However, the International Union for Conservation of Nature and Natural Resources (IUCN) classifies the species' status as vulnerable because the population continues to decline in other areas of the bird's habitat. Without the conservation efforts and special protections that have been responsible for its preservation and growth in Europe, the Dalmatian pelican could become extinct elsewhere.

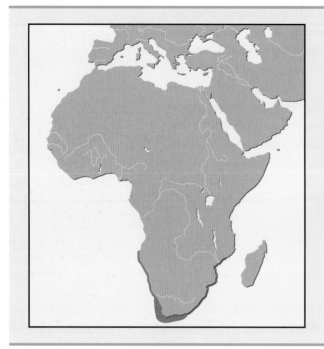

Penguin, African
Spheniscus demersus

PHYLUM: Chordata
CLASS: Aves
ORDER: Sphenisciformes
FAMILY: Spheniscidae
STATUS: Endangered, IUCN
Endangered, ESA
RANGE: Angola, Mozambique, Namibia, South Africa

Penguin, African
Spheniscus demersus

Description and biology

Like other penguin species, the African penguin displays distinctive black-and-white markings. Its black back contrasts with a white chest speckled with black. It has black cheeks. Above the eyes is a white stripe stretching down the neck. Naked patches of skin above the eyes help the bird handle a warmer habitat than most other penguin species can tolerate. In hot weather, blood rushes to these patches, turning them bright pink. This action throws off excess body heat. Adult birds measure between 23.5 and 27.5 inches (60 and 70 centimeters) long, with a weight ranging from 4.6 to 8.2 pounds (2.1 to 3.7 kilograms). This species makes a braying noise like a donkey, earning it the name *jackass penguin*.

The African penguin spends most of its time in the ocean, hunting for sardines, anchovies, and squid. Its flightless wings make good flip-

The African penguin, found along the coastline of southern Africa, must compete for food with commercial fishers who work in the waters of it habitat. © SERGEY URYADNIKOV/SHUTTERSTOCK.COM.

pers, propelling the bird through the water as fast as 12.4 miles (20 kilometers) an hour. It dives for about two and a half minutes at a time, reaching depths of up to 98 feet (30 meters). When feeding their young, African penguins stay close to shore. Otherwise, adults generally travel up to 250 miles (400 kilometers) away from their breeding site over a four-month period before returning to breed.

These penguins mate for life. They breed year-round, usually at the same spot. The species formerly burrowed into its guano (feces) when nesting, which shielded the young from heat and predators. Throughout the 20th century, however, people removed the guano to use for fertil-izer. Now the birds must nest in open sand or under boulders or bushes. Females lay two eggs, which both parents take turns incubating (sitting on or brooding). For the chicks' first month of life, both parents guard the nest. Chicks remain in groups onshore for several more months. They then leave the breeding site, traveling up to 620 miles (1,000 kilo-meters) away before returning to the breeding site two years later. Afri-can penguins usually live for 10 to 27 years.

Habitat and current distribution

African penguins breed on 25 islands and 4 mainland sites in Namibia and South Africa. They also swim near the coasts of Angola and Mo-zambique. The total population is 75,000 to 80,000, with the adult pop-ulation being 52,000.

History and conservation measures

African penguins evolved from ancestors whose fossils date back 10 mil-lion to 12 million years. Europeans first encountered the birds in 1497, when Portuguese explorer Vasco da Gama sailed into a South African bay. Da Gama's crew marveled at the braying noises and the flightless-ness of these unusual birds, the first penguins any Europeans had seen. In 1900 more than 1.5 million African penguins lived in South Africa. But the population dropped rapidly throughout the 20th century be-cause of guano collection, leaving the birds to nest in less suitable loca-tions. Biologists (people who study living organisms) estimate that the population has decreased by 90 percent since 1930.

Between 2004 and 2012, the African penguin population in South Africa declined by 10 percent each year. The biggest reason for this recent decline is a decrease in the supply of sardines and anchovies, the African penguin's preferred food. Overfishing has severely reduced the sardine and anchovy population off the Namibian coast. Off the South African coast, sardines and anchovies are now spawning (laying eggs) farther east than before, beyond the penguins' fishing range. Climate change may also have caused the fish to move. Oil spills present another hazard be-cause the birds breed near major ports where oil tankers dock. In 2000 conservationists (people who work to manage and protect nature) cleaned or relocated 38,000 birds after a spill. Most of the penguins survived.

South Africa has taken many measures to protect African penguins. All breeding sites are protected, guano collection is banned, and a government-funded program cleans birds harmed by oil spills. This program also educates people about the birds and installs artificial nests that protect chicks from heat and predators. Besides these actions, conservationists recommend banning fishing near breeding islands, protecting breeding sites in Namibia, and establishing captive-breeding programs.

Penguin, yellow-eyed
Megadyptes antipodes

PHYLUM: Chordata
CLASS: Aves
ORDER: Sphenisciformes
FAMILY: Spheniscidae
STATUS: Endangered, IUCN
Threatened, ESA
RANGE: New Zealand

Penguin, yellow-eyed
Megadyptes antipodes

Description and biology

Penguins are flightless sea birds. Like other penguins, the yellow-eyed penguin is mainly gray and white in color. What separates this penguin from others is its striking crown of yellow feathers and its bright, yellow eyes. Its cheeks are pale yellow, its bill is pink and red, and its feet are pink. In New Zealand, the yellow-eyed penguin is called the *hoiho*, a Maori word that means "noise shouter," because of the bird's shrill call.

An average adult yellow-eyed penguin can measure 30 inches (76 centimeters) long and weigh 11 pounds (5 kilograms). Its torpedo-shaped body allows the bird to travel swiftly in water, where it catches squid, crustaceans (shellfish such as shrimp and crabs), and small fish. On land, the penguin shuffles along on well-used paths from the sea to grassy cliffs and inland forests. It often walks more than 0.5 miles (0.8 kilometers) a day.

The yellow-eyed penguin is less social compared to other penguin species, which are normally very social. It may live in colonies made up of only a few birds or as many as 50 pairs. Penguins tend to mate for life. The breeding season for yellow-eyed penguins lasts only from late September to mid-October. Their nests, made of sticks and coarse grass, are located in holes in the ground, among rocks, or within stunted trees or shrubs.

A female yellow-eyed penguin lays two eggs, the second of which is laid 4 days after the first. Both parents incubate (sit on or brood) the eggs for about 42 days. Upon birth, the chicks are covered in fine, short, dark brown feathers. As they grow older, their distinctive yellow crown begins to emerge. When they are about six weeks old, the chicks are left alone in the nest, and they may venture out to sea shortly thereafter. Fewer than 20 percent of yellow-eyed penguin chicks survive into adulthood, being more vulnerable to dangers such as predators and disease when they are young.

Habitat and current distribution

The yellow-eyed penguin is found in New Zealand on South, Stewart, Codfish, Campbell, and Auckland Islands. Biologists (people who study living organisms) estimate that fewer than 7,000 of these penguins existed as of 2009. Of these, they believe that there are only about 1,600 breeding pairs.

The birds prefer to inhabit coastal waters. They feed in inshore waters and roost (rest or sleep) on sandy beaches.

History and conservation measures

The primary threat to the yellow-eyed penguin has been the disturbance or destruction of its nesting habitat. Much of it has been converted into farmland. Other areas have been degraded or worn down by grazing livestock from nearby farms. Predators that have been brought into the area by humans—especially ferrets, weasels, cats, and pigs—have also taken their toll on the bird's population.

Yellow-eyed penguins have also suffered at the hands of fishers. The birds often become tangled in fishing nets, and many have died as a result. Pesticides and other forms of pollution have killed many yellow-eyed penguins by contaminating their food sources. The penguins are also threatened by bacterial and parasitic diseases.

The yellow-eyed penguin has experienced threats to its breeding areas from predators, disease, and human activity that put its population at risk. © SHAUN JEFFERS/SHUTTERSTOCK.COM.

Wildlife organizations in New Zealand have purchased nesting sites to preserve what remains of the yellow-eyed penguin's habitat. Within these sites, conservationists (people who work to manage and protect nature) have removed introduced predators and have begun to replant trees and other types of vegetation (plant life). New Zealand adopted a conservation plan for the yellow-eyed penguin in 2000. The government hopes to significantly increase the population of the species and community involvement in its preservation by 2025. In 2010 the yellow-eyed penguin was added as a threatened species to the U.S. Endangered Species List, which includes threatened and endangered species from around the world.

Pheasant, cheer
Catreus wallichii

PHYLUM: Chordata
CLASS: Aves
ORDER: Galliformes
FAMILY: Phasianidae
STATUS: Vulnerable, IUCN
Endangered, ESA
RANGE: India, Nepal, Pakistan

Pheasant, cheer
Catreus wallichii

Description and biology

Cheer pheasants have brown crests, red-skinned faces, buff-gray feathers with black markings, and long tails. Males and females have similar plumage (covering of feathers), but the female has less dramatic coloring. The tail of the male cheer pheasant measures 18 to 24 inches (46 to 61 centimeters) long and is marked with heavy, dark bars. The male has an overall length of 35 to 47 inches (89 to 119 centimeters). Females are smaller, measuring 24 to 30 inches (61 to 76 centimeters) in length, with tails that are 12.5 to 18.5 inches (32 to 47 centimeters) long. This pheasant is mainly vegetarian (plant-eating), but also eats beetles, snails, insect larvae, and worms. It digs for roots and seeds with its stout feet and beak. It also plucks at leaves, shoots, and berries on the ground or in shrubs.

Breeding takes place in the spring. A male-female pair and one of their young male offspring defend a territory of 38 to 100 acres (15 to

The cheer pheasant is at risk in its native India, Pakistan, and Nepal, where increasing human populations and agricultural development are shrinking its habitat. It is also a target for hunters. © KRYS BAILEY/ALAMY.

40 hectares). This territory is often called the "crowing area" because of the sound the males make at dawn and dusk as a sign of defense. After building a shallow nest on the ground among boulders or stunted shrubs, a female cheer pheasant lays a clutch (number of eggs produced at one time) of 8 to 10 eggs. She then incubates (sits on or broods) the eggs for 26 to 28 days. After hatching, the chicks stay with their parents until the following spring. When not breeding, cheer pheasant families may come together to form flocks of 5 to 15 birds.

Habitat and current distribution

The cheer pheasant is found in the western Himalayas (mountain range) in Pakistan, northern India, and Nepal. The pheasant inhabits grassy hillsides with scattered patches of oak and pine. It is found most commonly at elevations between 4,740 and 10,000 feet (1,445 and 3,050 meters). It is often found grazing close to hill villages.

Biologists (people who study living organisms) estimated in 2012 that there were only between 3,000 and 4,000 cheer pheasants in existence throughout the species' habitat area.

History and conservation measures

Because cheer pheasants are found in groups that stay in one place, they are easily hunted. Despite having legal protection throughout their range, the birds are widely shot and trapped for food and to sell. People also eat cheer pheasant eggs. Many of the bird's populations in India live outside protected areas. Cheer pheasants have also suffered because cattle graze on their habitat and farmers often burn their grassy hillsides to create cleared land for farming.

In Pakistan, the pheasant survives only in the Jhelum Valley. In the past the bird could be found in a number of protected areas in the country, including the Salkhala Game Reserve and Machiara National Park, but as of 2012 scientists have reported no evidence of the bird in those areas. A program in the 1980s to reintroduce captive-born pheasants into the Margalla Hills National Park—another former habitat of the bird—was not successful.

A captive-breeding program, Cheer Pheasant Conservation Breeding Project, has been started in northern India to increase the species' population. It has successfully bred at least 50 pheasants in captivity and as of 2015 was still working on a plan to release them. Conservationists (people who work to manage and protect nature) believe that additional programs are still needed to preserve the animal's habitat, reduce poaching (illegal hunting), and increase public awareness about the plight of the cheer pheasant.

Plover, piping
Charadrius melodus

PHYLUM: Chordata
CLASS: Aves
ORDER: Charadriiformes
FAMILY: Charadriidae
STATUS: Near threatened, IUCN
Endangered, ESA (Great
Lakes region and Mississippi)
Threatened, ESA (elsewhere)
RANGE: Bahamas, Barbados, Bermuda, British Virgin Islands, Canada,
Cuba, Dominican Republic, Guadeloupe, Haiti, Jamaica, Martinique,
Mexico, Nicaragua, Puerto Rico, Saint
Kitts and Nevis, Saint Pierre and Miquelon, Turks and Caicos Islands, USA, U.S.
Virgin Islands

Plover, piping
Charadrius melodus

Description and biology

The piping plover is so-named because of its distinctive call, a two-note
piping or peeping sound. The color of this shore bird's plumage (covering of feathers) is sandy beige above and white below. It has a short black
bill and yellow legs. During breeding season, the piping plover develops
black markings on its forehead and throat. Its bill turns orange, except
at the tip, which remains black. Its legs also turn bright orange. The average piping plover is 7 inches (18 centimeters) long and weighs 1.5 to
2.2 ounces (42.5 to 62 grams).

This bird's diet includes insects and small marine animals such as
crawfish, snails, and clams. It locates its food by following the backwash
of waves, which deposit or uncover these animals on beaches. The bird's
predators include raccoons, foxes, opossums, gulls, skunks, rats, and feral (once domesticated, now wild) cats and dogs.

Breeding season takes place between March and August. The male piping plover courts the female with both aerial (flying) and ground displays or movements. After having mated, the female lays a clutch (number of eggs produced at one time) of 4 eggs in a shallow hollow in the ground lined with pebbles or plant debris. Both the male and female incubate (sit on or brood) the eggs for about 30 days. The chicks fledge (develop flying feathers) approximately 30 days after they hatch.

Habitat and current distribution

The piping plover is found on open beaches and sand and mud flats in North America. It breeds primarily in three regions: the Atlantic coast from southern Canada to North Carolina, along rivers and wetlands (areas where there is a lot of water in the soil, such as swamps or tidal flats) in the Great Plains from southern Canada to Nebraska, and the western

The piping plover, native to North America, has seen its population rebound after conservation and protection programs were enacted in the 1990s. © PAUL REEVES PHOTOGRAPHY/SHUTTERSTOCK.COM.

Great Lakes. In winter, the bird migrates to coastal areas and sand flats from the Carolinas south to Yucatán, Mexico. It also migrates to the Bahamas and the islands of the West Indies.

Biologists (people who study living organisms) estimated in 2012 that there were between 12,000 and 13,000 piping plovers in existence.

History and conservation measures

The piping plover was almost certainly more plentiful at the beginning of the 20th century than it is today. The earliest cause of the bird's decline was excessive hunting in the early 1900s. Later in the century, disturbance and destruction of the bird's beach habitats became its main threats. The population of piping plovers declined significantly after the 1950s.

Because the piping plover nests on open coastal beaches, it is easily disturbed by humans and their pets. In addition, the bird has lost much of its nesting area as beaches and other waterfronts have been converted into recreational and living areas for humans. This has been especially true in the Great Lakes region of the United States.

Many conservation efforts to protect the piping plover's nesting areas are in process. These include restricting the use of off-road vehicles on beaches and building barriers around nests to prevent contact by humans and predators. Piping plovers bred in captivity are also added to populations in the Great Lakes area. Since 1991 the numbers of piping plovers in the wild have increased because of conservation programs. As a result, the International Union for Conservation of Nature and Natural Resources (IUCN) downlisted the piping plover from a status of vulnerable to near threatened in 2001 but warns that their continued success depends on maintaining conservation efforts.

Quetzal, resplendent
Pharomachrus mocinno

PHYLUM: Chordata
CLASS: Aves
ORDER: Trogoniformes
FAMILY: Trogonidae
STATUS: Near threatened, IUCN
Endangered, ESA
RANGE: Costa Rica, El Salvador, Guatemala, Honduras, Mexico, Nicaragua, Panama

Quetzal, resplendent
Pharomachrus mocinno

Description and biology

The resplendent quetzal (pronounced ket-SAL) is a stunning forest bird, considered to be among the most beautiful in the Western Hemisphere. Although both males and females have crested feathers on their heads and brilliant green upperparts, the color of the plumage (covering of feathers) on the rest of the body differs. Females have brown breasts and bellies and fairly short, black-and-white tails. Males have orange-red breasts and bellies. Their magnificent, 3-foot-long (1-meter-long) tail is the same shimmering green color as their upper body. An average adult quetzal measures 13.75 to 15 inches (35 to 38 centimeters) in length.

The quetzal feeds mainly on plants in the laurel family, but it also eats insects, small frogs, lizards, and snails. It usually stays in the canopy

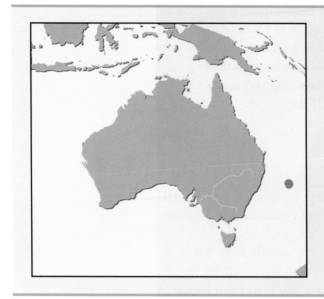

Rail, Lord Howe wood
Gallirallus sylvestris (also *Hypotaenidia sylvestris*)

PHYLUM: Chordata
CLASS: Aves
ORDER: Gruiformes
FAMILY: Rallidae
STATUS: Endangered, IUCN
Endangered, ESA
RANGE: Australia (Lord Howe Island)

Rail, Lord Howe wood
Gallirallus sylvestris (also *Hypotaenidia sylvestris*)

Description and biology

The Lord Howe wood rail, also called the Lord Howe woodhen, is a flightless bird that averages 12.5 to 16.5 inches (32 to 42 centimeters) in length. The color of its plumage (covering of feathers) is brown. Dark brown and black stripes mark its wings. The bird has a strong, curved bill and red eyes.

The wood rail feeds on worms, grubs, and insects. The bird is also highly territorial and works with its mate to defend its home area. Once it has established its territory, the wood rail rarely moves farther than 1,640 feet (500 meters) in any given direction. Owls that were introduced in the bird's habitat and feral (once domesticated, now wild) pigs are its main predators.

Lord Howe wood rails mate for life, and a male-female pair often remain apart from other wood rails. They begin reproduction at the end of winter and a female may lay several clutches (eggs produced at one time) throughout the spring season and into early summer. After building a nest on the ground, a female wood rail lays a clutch of one to four eggs. Biologists (people who study living organisms) estimate that it takes 20 to 23 days for the eggs to hatch. Upon hatching, the chicks are darker than the adults, and they fledge (develop flying feathers) once they are 28 days old.

Habitat and current distribution

The Lord Howe wood rail is found on Lord Howe Island, a remnant of an extinct volcano about 435 miles (700 kilometers) off the coast of the southeastern Australian state of New South Wales. The bird inhabits both lowland palm forests and mountain forests.

The species' population has improved since the 1970s and reached the island's carrying capacity, which means that Lord Howe Island cannot support any more wood rails than the 220 to 230 that already live there as of 2013.

Did You Know?

Biologists (people who study living organisms) estimate that there are only 220 to 230 Lord Howe wood rails left. However, it is most likely impossible for this population to increase, as scientists believe the species has reached the carrying capacity of its island. As any area has only a certain amount of land and food available for the animals, there comes a point for any species where the land cannot support more individuals. If the rails have a large number of offspring, the sudden competition for food and space will cause many birds to starve to death until eventually the population settles back at 220 to 230.

History and conservation measures

When English explorers first set foot on Lord Howe Island in 1788, the wood rail was found throughout the island. Not long after, English whaling ships began stopping at the island. The flightless wood rail had no fear of humans and could be easily captured; it thus became a prime food source for sailors. By the 1850s the English had established permanent settlements on the island. In time, some of the goats and pigs the English had brought with them to the island escaped from farms and became feral. They quickly killed off many of the remaining wood rails or seriously disturbed their habitat. By the beginning of the 20th century, the birds existed in low numbers only on the island's mountaintops.

By the mid-1970s biologists believed that the Lord Howe wood rail population numbered fewer than 30 birds. Conservationists (people who work to manage and protect nature) then began taking steps to eliminate introduced predators, such as the wild pig. In 1980 a captive-breeding

The Lord Howe wood rail is a flightless bird native to the forests of Lord Howe Island, Australia. © KEVIN SCHAFER/MINDEN PIC-
TURES/CORBIS.

program was initiated using three of the remaining wood rail pairs. The birds reproduced rapidly, and over the next four years, 85 birds bred in captivity were released into the wild. By 1990 the wild wood rail population had increased to about 50 breeding pairs and almost 200 total birds. Since 1997 the population has remained stable between 220 and 230 individual birds.

Even with the success of captive breeding, introduced species remain a threat to the wood rail. Of these, a major threat is the masked owl, introduced to the island in the 1920s to contain the black rat population. Modern methods of rat control using poisoned bait also threaten the rail. Current conservation efforts to save the Lord Howe wood rail are focused on controlling these predators. In addition, conservationists are working to establish a population of wood rails elsewhere from Lord Howe Island. This would reduce the risk of extinction, which remains high because the species' range is limited to a small island.

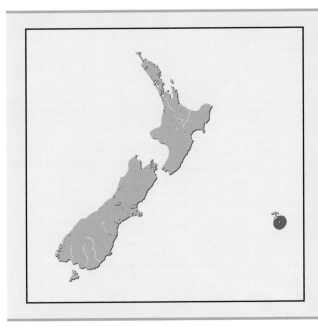

Robin, Chatham Island
Petroica traversi

PHYLUM: Chordata
CLASS: Aves
ORDER: Passeriformes
FAMILY: Petroicidae
STATUS: Endangered, IUCN
Endangered, ESA
RANGE: New Zealand (Chatham
Islands)

Robin, Chatham Island
Petroica traversi

Description and biology

The Chatham Island robin (also known as the black robin) is a species closely related to the New Zealand robin. It has coal black feathers, legs, feet, and bill. The adult robin is about 6 inches (15 centimeters) tall and weighs just 0.8 ounces (22.7 grams). It is similar in size to a sparrow but has longer legs. Females are a little smaller than males. The Chatham Island robin has dark brown eyes that provide excellent vision for hunting in the dark. It hunts for food both day and night, foraging through the litter (dead leaves and twigs) on the forest floor for worms, grubs, cockroaches, and particularly for an insect related to the grasshopper called the weta.

Chatham Island robins are noted for their song, which fills the forests around them during breeding season. They fly only short distances, from branch to branch, and stay in the lower branches of the forests in

The Chatham Island robin has bounced back from a dangerously low population in 1980 due to conservation and protection programs. © MARK CARWARDINE/PHOTOLIBRARY/GETTY IMAGES.

order to avoid the strong winds that blow over the islands. They are territorial animals, particularly during breeding season, and will protect their home areas from other birds of their species. They can live up to 14 years.

Chatham Island robins are usually monogamous—they stay with the same breeding partner throughout their lives. When it is breeding time, the female makes a nest in a hollow tree or tree stump and usually lays two eggs each year. The female incubates (sits on or broods) the eggs and the male brings her food. The eggs hatch in about 18 days and the chicks begin to fly and leave the nest after 3 weeks. The parents continue to feed the chicks for a couple of months after they hatch, long after they leave the nest.

Habitat and current distribution

Chatham Island robins live in the lower altitudes of a scrub-forest habitat. The birds are only found on two islands in New Zealand's Chatham Islands group. The largest population is on South East Island (also called Rangatira), which is only about 0.8 square miles (2 square kilometers) in area. A smaller population lives in Mangere Island, which has an area of about 0.4 square miles (1 square kilometer).

Biologists (people who study living organisms) counted a total of 281 birds on the two islands in 2011.

History and conservation measures

The Chatham Island robin has virtually come back from extinction and is regarded as one of the tremendous success stories in conservation (protecting nature). However, there is much to be done before the species is out of trouble.

The range of the robin once included most of the Chatham Islands. When Europeans arrived in New Zealand in the mid-19th century, they began clearing the forests and destroying the habitats vital to the species. They also introduced rats and cats, predators to the robin. By 1880 the range of the Chatham Island robin was severely reduced, and the species existed only on Little Mangere Island.

By the late 1970s there were only seven known birds left to represent the entire species. Because the habitat on Little Mangere had been badly damaged, scientists very carefully moved these last seven robins to Mangere Island. The birds were given a home in a forest that had been newly replanted, where the habitat was protected. For several years no mating took place and, by 1981, two of the seven birds had died. Only one female Chatham Island robin remained in the world. Her name was "Old Blue" (named after the color of the band that scientists had placed on her leg in order to track her). The future of the species seemed doomed.

Then, a group of scientists with the New Zealand Wildlife Service (now the Department of Conservation) set up a black robin recovery project on the islands. When Old Blue mated with one of the remaining males, "Old Yellow," her eggs were placed in the nests of Chatham Island tomtit females on South East Island, which became foster parents to the robin chicks. This project produced many new young that were returned to Mangere Island, though some were kept on South East Island to begin a new population there. By 1999 the two locations, Mangere and South East Island, were home to about 259 Chatham Island robins, and plans were underway to open more critical habitat for the species. In these areas, there are no predators and the habitat is restored.

The spectacular recovery, from 5 to at least 281 birds, is overshadowed by the fact that all of the new population stems from a single breeding pair, Old Blue and Old Yellow. Because of this, the gene base (the number of biological units that pass on hereditary traits) of the species is very limited. So far, this has not been a problem for the new and growing populations, but because all the birds in the species will have similar weaknesses, a newly introduced predator or disease could drastically reduce the populations again.

New Zealand continues to work on the species recovery and hopes to reintroduce the bird to its previous habitat on the island of Little Mangere.

Sage grouse, Gunnison
Centrocercus minimus

PHYLUM: Chordata
CLASS: Aves
ORDER: Galliformes
FAMILY: Phasianidae
STATUS: Endangered, IUCN
Threatened, ESA
RANGE: Colorado, Utah

Sage grouse, Gunnison
Centrocercus minimus

Description and biology

The name of the Gunnison sage grouse tells this species' story. The bird lives in the Gunnison Valley of Colorado, eats and nests in sagebrush, and is closely related to a more common species, the greater sage grouse (*Centrocercus urophasianus*). Gunnison sage grouse are about 22 inches (56 centimeters) long, with a wingspan of around 30 inches (76 centimeters), and weigh 2 to 5 pounds (1 to 2.2 kilograms). Males are more colorful than females, with a black head and belly, a gray-brown body, a fluffy white chest, and a black-and-white striped tail. During mating season, males expose yellow air sacs on their chests. Females are speckled gray, brown, and white with a black belly and black spots on their sides.

This species lives at elevations of about 7,000 feet (2,134 meters), in a valley with little rainfall. In summer, winter, and fall, the birds forage (search for food) in flocks. They eat mostly sagebrush in the fall and

The Gunnison sage grouse is found in only a very small area of Colorado and Utah. Here, a male Gunnison sage grouse displays its filoplumes (bulging air sacs) while trying to attract a mate. © HELEN H. RICHARDSON/THE DENVER POST/GETTY IMAGES.

winter, being able to digest the tough plant. During the summer, they eat other plants, as well as insects. The birds can fly but do not migrate, usually remaining within several miles of their home range.

Every March and April, males gather together in small areas called leks in order to attract females. Females choose only one or two of the males in the group for mating. After mating, females nest in the sage-brush near rivers. In late spring, they lay six to eight eggs, which hatch after about 27 days. Chicks become independent of their mothers at 10 to 12 weeks, but less than half survive. This species has a life span of three to nine years.

Habitat and current distribution

The Gunnison sage grouse inhabits 11 counties in southwestern Colorado and southeastern Utah. About 85 percent of the population lives in the Gunnison basin, a large valley in southwestern Colorado. Six small, scattered populations have been documented elsewhere in the state and in Utah. In 2014 the population was about 4,700 birds.

History and conservation measures

The Plains Indians have lived near sage grouse for thousands of years, mimicking their mating behavior in ceremonial dances and hunting them for food. Biologists (people who study living organisms) recognized the Gunnison sage grouse as a separate species from the greater sage grouse only in 2000. The species' population is declining because of habitat loss, fragmentation (breaking up of habitat into smaller areas that no longer border each other), and degradation (human destruction of habitat). Roads, reservoirs, real estate developments, power lines, cropland, and livestock grazing areas cover the land where Gunnison sage grouse used to live. The birds now occupy only 7 percent of their historical range. Small population size, drought, climate change, and disease are also threats.

The International Union for Conservation of Nature and Natural Resources (IUCN) listed the bird as endangered in 2012. Two years later, the U.S. Fish and Wildlife Service determined that the species is threatened according to the U.S. Endangered Species Act. This designation means that the species is protected on U.S. land and that private landowners who own land where grouse live cannot take actions that would negatively affect the species. Counties, Native American groups, and nonprofit organizations are working to conserve the Gunnison sage grouse, too. Actions being undertaken by these governmental and nongovernmental organizations include restoring areas near nesting sites, protecting lek sites, and educating the public about the species.

Did You Know?

Sage grouse are known for their mating behavior. They are a lekking species, which is common for game birds such as grouse, prairie chickens, and peafowl. The lek refers to a small area, usually a clearing such as an opening in the brush, where a group of male birds gathers together to attract females. Before and after sunrise, the males strut around, jerking their heads and spreading out and shaking their tails. They puff up their chests and make popping, burbling noises. As they defend their territories within the lek, their object is to mate with as many females as possible. Usually only a few of the lekking males will mate with the surrounding females. Females choose only one or two of the males in the lek for mating, often seeking out the most dominant ones. Once mating is complete, the males have no contact with the females or chicks.

Spatuletail, marvelous
Loddigesia mirabilis

PHYLUM: Chordata
CLASS: Aves
ORDER: Apodiformes
FAMILY: Trochilidae
STATUS: Endangered, IUCN
RANGE: Peru

Spatuletail, marvelous
Loddigesia mirabilis

Description and biology

The marvelous spatuletail is a hummingbird native to Peru. The male has only four tail feathers—a unique feature among birds. Two of the feathers are shorter, and the outer two are elongated. The long tail feathers each end in spectacular spatules, or violet-blue discs. During mating, the male waves his tail feathers independently and vigorously as he beats his wings rapidly to hover in front of the female.

In addition to its tail, the male hummingbird can be identified by its blue cap or crest, a blue throat, and a white breast with a black line down its center. Its sides are green and its back and top are mostly bronze or brown. The females have a white throat and lack the line on their underside. They have much shorter tails, though like the male their two longer tail feathers end in discs or spatules.

The marvelous spatuletail has two long tail feathers that each end in spatules, or violet-blue discs. During mating season, the male waves its tail feathers independently and vigorously as he hovers near the female. © ALL CANADA PHOTOS/ALAMY.

Hummingbirds feed on nectar from flowers, which they lap up with their tongues. The marvelous spatuletail feeds on a number of flowering plants, though its preferred food is the nectar of the red-flowered lily *Alstroemeria (Bomarea) formosissima*.

Much about the habits and behavior of the spatuletail is unknown, but it is thought to breed from late October to early May. The males gather in groups, called leks, in order to put on their courtship displays.

Habitat and current distribution

The marvelous spatuletail has only been recorded in and around the Cordillera de Colán National Sanctuary in the Bagua and Utcubamba Provinces of northern Peru. The population is estimated at 350 to 1,500 individuals.

The pet trade has severely diminished the wild populations of the Rothschild's starling of Bali, Indonesia, although birds raised in captivity have been released in its habitat in hopes of increasing the species' numbers. © NAGEL PHOTOGRAPHY/ SHUTTERSTOCK.COM.

Habitat and current distribution

Rothschild's starling is found on Bali, an Indonesian island off the eastern end of the larger island of Java. The starling is restricted to the remaining woodland in the northwestern coastal area of the island, most of which is situated within West Bali National Park. A separate wild population, created entirely from captive-bred individuals, has been introduced on Nusa Penida (an island southeast of Bali). It is unclear exactly how many starlings remain in the wild, but a 2008 report estimated the number on Bali to be around 50. Although at least 65 adult and 62 young starlings were present on Nusa Penida in 2009, only 12 were found in a count on the island conducted in 2015.

History and conservation measures

The greatest threat to Rothschild's starling is illegal trapping. The beauty of the bird has made it highly prized by private collectors. It is legally protected in Indonesia and is listed on Appendix I of the Convention on International Trade in Endangered Species of Wild Fauna and Flora (CITES; an international treaty to protect wildlife), meaning that international trade of the species is prohibited (except in extraordinary circumstances). Despite the protections, poachers (illegal hunters) continue to capture and export the bird for profit.

The parks protecting the birds from international trade have also suffered from mismanagement and corruption, increasing the species' risk of extinction. For example, in 1999 an armed gang stole the 39 captive starlings in West Bali National Park that were intended to be released into the wild. According to the International Union for Conservation of Nature and Natural Resources (IUCN), the price at the time for Rothschild's starlings on the black market (where goods are traded illegally) was almost $2,000 per bird, a high incentive for the theft. Furthermore, much of the starling's habitat has been lost, as forests have been cleared to create farmland.

Conservation programs are in place to help the species recover, including introduction of captive-bred specimens into the wild. Rothschild's starling breeds well in captivity, and it is thought that there are almost 1,000 individuals in captivity worldwide. Breeding the birds for reintroduction efforts (efforts to introduce animals in captivity back into the wild) has been a primary goal of conservation programs, and the Wildlife Conservation Society is monitoring black-market trade of the starling at key locations in Indonesia. Despite the work done to help save the species, however, the Rothschild's starling remains critically endangered.

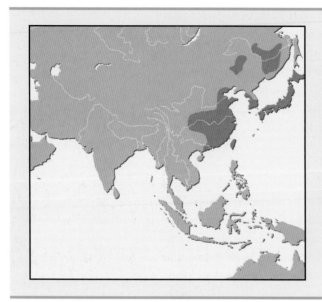

Stork, Oriental white
Ciconia boyciana

PHYLUM: Chordata
CLASS: Aves
ORDER: Ciconiiformes
FAMILY: Ciconiidae
STATUS: Endangered, IUCN
Endangered, ESA
RANGE: China, Japan, North Korea,
Russia, South Korea

Stork, Oriental white
Ciconia boyciana

Description and biology

The Oriental white stork is also known as the Japanese white stork and the Far Eastern white stork. With a body length of 43 to 45 inches (110 to 115 centimeters) and a wingspan of about 46 inches (118 centimeters), it is bigger than its cousin, the European white stork. It has a distinctive black bill and long white wings with black tips. Male Oriental white storks, weighing about 11 pounds (5 kilograms), are larger than females, which weigh about 10 pounds (4.5 kilograms).

The Oriental white stork's diet is made up of insects, fish, frogs, snails, small reptiles, and small mammals, such as rodents. The stork is a migratory bird, traveling very long distances to relocate seasonally. It tends to be quite aggressive with other members of its species.

Breeding male and female Oriental white storks make their nests in sections of the forest as far away from human communities as possible. The nests are made from branches and straw and are about 6.5 feet

(2 meters) in diameter. The female stork usually lays about four or five eggs. Then the male and the female take turns incubating, or sitting on, the eggs to keep them warm. When the chicks are born, both parents feed them by regurgitating (vomiting) undigested food into their

The Oriental white stork is at risk because of the effects of deforestation and wetland destruction on its habitat in Asia. © FEATHERCOLLECTOR/ SHUTTERSTOCK.COM.

mouths. The young leave the nest after about 65 days and begin to find their own food. In captivity an Oriental white stork lives about 48 years.

Habitat and current distribution

The Oriental white stork currently breeds in the basins of the Amur and Ussuri Rivers in southeastern Russia and northeastern China. These storks migrate each winter. Most travel a distance of about 1,865 miles (3,000 kilometers) to spend the winter in the Yangtze (Chang) River valley in China. Small numbers of the stork also winter in Japan, North Korea, and South Korea. The total population of Oriental white storks in the world was estimated to be fewer than 2,500 mature birds as of 2013.

The Oriental white stork prefers to live in open, freshwater wetlands (areas where there is a lot of water in the soil, such as swamps or tidal flats). It nests on tall trees and sometimes on tall human-made structures, such as the poles of electric power lines.

History and conservation measures

The Oriental white stork once had a large range in Asia. It became extinct as a breeding species in Japan in 1959 and in North and South Korea in 1971. In the past, Oriental white storks spent winters in India, Myanmar, and Bangladesh, but the species is now rarely seen in those countries.

The reasons for the decline in the Oriental white stork population are human related. The trees that the storks nest in have been cleared and the wetlands (areas where there is a lot of water in the soil, such as swamps or tidal flats) where they find their food have been drained. In Japan and the Koreas, people hunted the birds until the population had totally vanished from those countries. Pollution has probably further reduced the number. In China the building of the Three Gorges Dam on the Yangtze River and other hydroelectric projects (which create electricity from water power) are expected to have a heavy impact on the Oriental white stork's habitat. In Russia the development of wetlands for farming has crowded the birds into increasingly smaller regions.

Russia, China, South Korea, and Japan have enacted laws protecting the Oriental white stork. There are a number of protected breeding and wintering areas in Russia and China. Oriental white storks have been bred in captivity, and there are reintroduction programs in South Korea and Japan. As of 2008, there were about 100 birds in Hyogo Prefecture, Japan, after chicks bred in Russia were reintroduced there.

Conservationists (people who work to manage and protect nature) are studying ways to increase the species' protected habitats and to create better habitats for the storks by planting elm trees near their feeding areas. One of the great difficulties in conservation with this species is its migratory (relocating) habits: its welfare depends on the abilities of several countries to work together with one another to protect it.

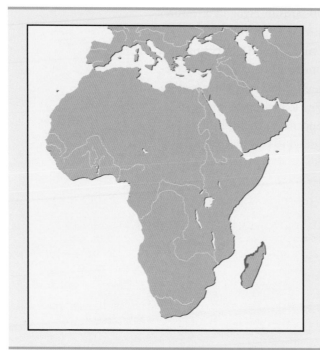

Teal, Madagascar
Anas bernieri

PHYLUM: Chordata
CLASS: Aves
ORDER: Anseriformes
FAMILY: Anatidae
STATUS: Endangered, IUCN
RANGE: Madagascar

Teal, Madagascar
Anas bernieri

Description and biology

The Madagascar teal, also known as Bernier's teal, is a small duck of about 16 inches (40 centimeters) in length, weighing about 1 pound (450 grams). The plumage (covering of feathers) is brownish gray, and there is a black-and-white band on each wing. The feathers under the wing are gray with white edges. The Madagascar teal has a long neck, large eyes, and a light red bill.

The Madagascar teal is found in either freshwater or saltwater where there is abundant plant life and rich mud. Like all teals, it is a "dabbler" (rather than a diver); it feeds while wading in shallow waters less than 4 inches (10 centimeters) deep by sifting through the water and mud for invertebrate animals (animals with no backbone) and some water plant

The Madagascar teal's already limited population is further threatened by habitat loss and hunting. © STEPHEN MEESE/ SHUTTERSTOCK.COM.

seeds. The teal sifts for food throughout the day and night but prefers the early morning and early evening hours. It walks well on land and has wings large enough to fly very slowly.

Madagascar teals are monogamous: once a male and female mate, they stay together for life. Breeding takes place from December to March, the rainy season in Madagascar. The male and female build a nest, usually in a hole in a mangrove tree trunk. They are territorial and will defend their territory against other teals. The female produces about six eggs and incubates (sits on or broods) them for about a month. The male watches over the female carefully while she is tending the eggs. The ducklings are well developed when they hatch, covered in soft down and able to move about and eat by themselves. Within about six weeks from hatching they will be able to fly. When not breeding, groups of teals form small flocks. The female Madagascar teal makes a quacking call; the male makes a whistling sound.

The white-breasted thrasher perches on a branch in its native Saint Lucia. The bird is also found on the island of Martinique.
© FLPA/ALAMY.

time) of two to four greenish-blue eggs in a bulky nest made of twigs and leaves. Eggs hatch after 14 days, and chicks begin to fledge (develop flying feathers) when they are about 12 days old. The nest is often found 3.3 to 9.8 feet (1 to 3 meters) above the ground in young trees.

The white-breasted thrasher species is divided biologically into two subspecies: *Ramphocinclus brachyurus brachyurus* and *Ramphocinclus brachyurus sanctaeluciae*. The main physical difference between the two is color. The birds of the subspecies *brachyurus* are lighter than those of the subspecies *sanctaeluciae*.

Habitat and current distribution

The white-breasted thrasher is unique to the Caribbean islands of Martinique and Saint Lucia. Martinique is home to one population of the thrasher subspecies *Ramphocinclus brachyurus brachyurus*. Saint Lucia is home to two populations of the thrasher subspecies *Ramphocinclus brachyurus sanctaeluciae*. Biologists (people who study living organisms) estimate that there are about 1,900 white-breasted thrashers in existence.

White-breasted thrashers prefer to inhabit dense thickets in semiarid (partly or mostly dry) forests within 1.2 miles (2 kilometers) of the coast. The bird avoids open land and forest areas with tree canopies lower than 16.4 feet (5 meters).

History and conservation measures

The white-breasted thrasher is one of the rarest birds of the West Indies. Although considered quite common on Martinique and Saint Lucia in the 19th century, the bird was considered extinct by 1950. That same year, it was rediscovered on the Presqu'île de la Caravelle, a peninsula that juts 5 miles (8 kilometers) out from the island of Martinique into the Atlantic Ocean.

Habitat destruction on both Martinique and Saint Lucia has been, and continues to be, one of the major threats to the white-breasted thrasher. The bird is also threatened by introduced predators, such as mongooses and rats. The white-breasted thrasher is easy prey for these animals because it spends much time feeding on the ground and is not a strong flier.

On Martinique, the white-breasted thrasher's range lies within the Caravelle Natural Reserve. On Saint Lucia, none of the bird's range is within a protected area. A species action plan was developed in 2014 for Saint Lucia with the goal of increasing the species' population and managing at least three sites of the species' habitat, all by 2020.

Vireo, black-capped
Vireo atricapilla

PHYLUM: Chordata
CLASS: Aves
ORDER: Passeriformes
FAMILY: Vireonidae
STATUS: Vulnerable, IUCN
Endangered, ESA
RANGE: Mexico, USA (Oklahoma,
Texas)

Vireo, black-capped
Vireo atricapilla

Description and biology

The black-capped vireo (pronounced VEER-e-o), also called the black-capped greenlet, is a small songbird that averages about 4.7 inches (12 centimeters) in length. The color of the male's plumage (covering of feathers) is dull yellowish-green above and whitish below. The female is slightly darker above with yellowish underparts. The head is black in the male and gray in the female. Both have white eye markings. The bird forages in leaves and branches for insects, spiders, fruits, and seeds.

A female black-capped vireo lays a clutch (number of eggs produced at one time) of three to five eggs in a rounded nest made of vegetation (plants). Both the male and female take turns incubating (sitting on or brooding) the eggs for 14 to 17 days until they hatch. Snakes and scrub jays sometimes prey on the eggs or the young nestlings.

Habitat and current distribution

The black-capped vireo can be found in Oklahoma and in northern and western Texas. Biologists (people who study living organisms) are not sure, but there also may be populations in Mexico and southwestern Texas. Approximately 8,000 black-capped vireos are estimated to be in existence throughout the species' range.

The black-capped vireo requires a very special nesting habitat. It nests in shrubs on rocky slopes or eroded banks in areas between forests and grasslands.

History and conservation measures

The black-capped vireo once bred throughout the south-central United States, from Kansas south to Mexico, and wintered along the Pacific

A black-capped vireo feeding her nestlings. © RICK & NORA BOWERS/ALAMY.

Ocean. Over the years, much of the bird's habitat was converted into farms and urban areas. Other portions of its habitat were destroyed by the overgrazing of cattle and other livestock.

The changing of natural habitat by humans has affected the black-capped vireo in another serious way. The brown-headed cowbird normally inhabits grasslands and prairies. As its habitat has been taken over by humans, it has had to expand its range into that of the black-capped vireo. The cowbird likes to lay its eggs in the nests of smaller birds, such as vireos and sparrows. Once the cowbird nestlings hatch, they compete with the other nestlings for food from the new parents. Many times, the smaller nestlings die from starvation. In some areas, this type of behavior, called parasitism (pronounced PAIR-uh-suh-tiz-um), occurred in over 90 percent of black-capped vireo nests.

Scientists also have discovered that South American fire ants, accidentally brought into the black-capped vireo's range, are preying on the bird's nestlings. The ants attack the nest and devour the nestlings within the course of a single night. Snakes and mammals also feed on the nestlings of the black-capped vireo.

Current conservation measures on behalf of the vireo include controlling the cowbird population and protecting the vireo's habitat in a number of locations in both Oklahoma and Texas. Scientists are also conducting additional research on wintering and breeding areas in Mexico and the United States.

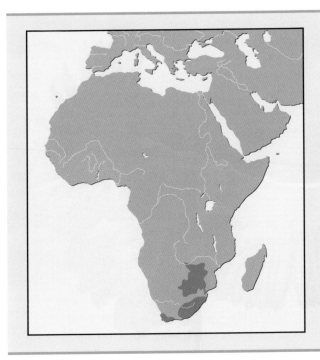

Vulture, Cape
Gyps coprotheres

PHYLUM: Chordata
CLASS: Aves
ORDER: Accipitriformes
FAMILY: Accipitridae
STATUS: Vulnerable, IUCN
RANGE: Angola, Botswana, Lesotho, Mozambique, South Africa, Zimbabwe

Vulture, Cape
Gyps coprotheres

Description and biology

The Cape vulture, also called the Cape griffon, is an Old World vulture that belongs to the same family as hawks and eagles. It is very large and measures between 39 and 45 inches (100 and 115 centimeters) in length. It has a long, bare neck and a specially shaped tongue that allows it to feed inside the carcasses (dead bodies) of sheep, cattle, pigs, goats, and horses. The bird roosts (rests or sleeps) with other vultures in colonies on cliffs. Unlike most birds of prey, the Cape vulture does not use thermals (rising warm air currents) to fly. Instead, it uses the swift air currents that exist around its roosting sites. The vulture used to eat the carcasses of large migratory mammals. Now, it must depend on dead livestock for food.

Cape vultures begin to build their nests in early March, constructing them within colonies of up to 1,000 breeding pairs. The nests are

463

from osteodystrophy and has slowed the decline in population numbers in some areas. The Cape vulture has full legal protection throughout its range.

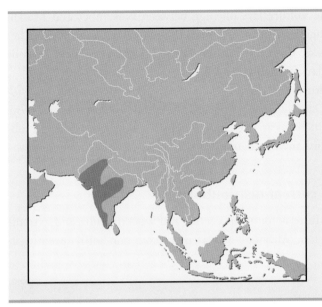

Vulture, Indian
Gyps indicus

PHYLUM: Chordata
CLASS: Aves
ORDER: Accipitriformes
FAMILY: Accipitridae
STATUS: Critically endangered, IUCN
RANGE: India, Pakistan

Vulture, Indian
Gyps indicus

Description and biology

The Indian vulture can be recognized by its pale bill and its black head and neck. It has pale down (soft feathers) on its head and neck and white ruffs (a ring of feathers) around its neck. Its back and upper wings are brown, with feathers turning to cream on the underside. The birds weigh 12 to 14 pounds (5.5 to 6.3 kilograms) and are 31 to 41 inches (80 to 103 centimeters) long and have a 6.4- to 7.8-foot (2- to 2.4-meter) wingspan.

The Indian vulture is a scavenger, meaning that it eats only carrion (the decaying flesh of dead animals). It is found in both rural settings and in urban areas, where it feeds from garbage dumps or slaughterhouses. The bird builds large nests, 2 to 3 feet (0.6 to 0.9 meters) in diameter, out of green leaves and garbage. The nests are usually located on cliffs or in ruins, although sometimes the birds will also build nests in trees. Indian vultures nest in small colonies.

The female vulture lays one egg between November and March. Both parents incubate (sit on or brood) the egg, which generally hatches after seven weeks. Both mother and father care for the chick. Juvenile vultures have dark bills and pinkish heads and necks.

Indian vultures are closely related to the griffon vulture (*Gyps fulvus*). Another closely related species, the slender-billed vulture (*Gyps tenuirostris*), which has an overlapping range, was once considered a subspecies of the Indian vulture but is now classified as a separate species.

Habitat and current distribution

The Indian vulture is found in central and western India and extreme southern Pakistan. Although it was quite common until recently, its

The Indian vulture has suffered a catastrophic population decline, which has reduced its numbers by as much as 95 percent.
© UNIVERSAL IMAGES GROUP LIMITED/ALAMY.

numbers have been greatly reduced. A rough estimate based on 2007 survey results suggest that within its range a total of 30,000 adults exist.

History and conservation measures

Indian vultures adapted easily to living with humans and were able to thrive in urban areas by eating refuse from garbage dumps and slaughterhouses. As a result, they did not suffer from habitat destruction, as many species have, and they were very common in South Asia up to the late 1990s.

Since that time, however, the vultures have suffered a catastrophic population decline, which has reduced their numbers by as much as 95 percent. In India's Keoladeo National Park, for example, bird counts dropped from 816 to just 25 between the mid-1980s and the late 1990s.

At first, scientists believed that the decline was the result of a viral infection. Further research showed, however, that birds were dying because of the drug diclofenac, used to treat domestic livestock. The drug causes kidney failure in vultures, who ingest it when feeding on livestock carcasses.

India, Pakistan, and other regional governments have passed laws banning or restricting diclofenac, although it may take some time for use of it to cease entirely. A replacement drug that works in cattle but does not affect vultures has also been developed. Captive-breeding sites have been established in the hopes that Indian vulture populations can be reestablished as diclofenac becomes less of a threat.

In the meantime, the loss of Indian vultures is having a negative effect on humans. With the decline in vulture population, carcasses are not disposed of as quickly. This can contribute to the spread of disease. It also has resulted in an increase in the population of feral (once domesticated, now wild) dogs, which is dangerous because dogs often carry rabies.

Warbler, Kirtland's
Setophaga kirtlandii (also *Dendroica kirtlandii*)

PHYLUM: Chordata
CLASS: Aves
ORDER: Passeriformes
FAMILY: Parulidae
STATUS: Near threatened, IUCN
Endangered, ESA
RANGE: Bahamas, Canada, Turks
and Caicos Islands, USA (Michigan,
Wisconsin)

Warbler, Kirtland's
Setophaga kirtlandii (also *Dendroica kirtlandii*)

Description and biology

Kirtland's warbler is a songbird that grows to an average length of 6 inches (15 centimeters). It has a blue-gray head and upper body with black streaks on its back. Its underside is pale yellow with darker streaks. Males have a black spot on their cheeks, whereas females have a gray one. Both sexes have incomplete white rings around their eyes. The Kirtland's warbler has a habit of bobbing its tail as it moves along the ground. The bird has been seen feeding on moths, caterpillars, ants, and numerous other insects, as well as on berries.

The Kirtland's warbler nests and breeds in a very specific habitat. It rejects deciduous forests (made up of trees whose leaves fall off annually) and areas that have dense underbrush. It chooses only areas at least 80 acres (32 hectares) in size with large stands of young jack pine on relatively level ground. These areas develop naturally only as a result

The Kirtland's warbler has experienced an increase in its population after conservation and protection programs were enacted beginning in the late 1980s. © NATURE PHOTOGRAPHERS LTD/ALAMY.

of intense forest fires. The warbler moves into the area 9 to 13 years after a fire has swept through, when the new jack pines are about 5 feet (1.5 meters) tall. After 6 to 12 years, when the pines have reached 12 to 18 feet (3.6 to 5.5 meters) in height, the warbler abandons the area for a new one.

The warbler builds a nest of grass, bark, and fibers on the ground beneath a jack pine. A female Kirtland's warbler lays three to five brown-speckled white eggs between mid-May and mid-July. She then incubates (sits on or broods) them for 10 to 14 days until they hatch.

Habitat and current distribution

The Kirtland's warbler breeds only in stands of young jack pine. Until 1995 its nesting area was limited to the Lower Peninsula of Michigan. But since then it has also been nesting in Wisconsin and Canada. Beginning in late September, the bird migrates to the Bahamas and the Turks and Caicos Islands, located at the southeastern end of the Bahamas. Its winter habitat consists mainly of pine woods. The warbler returns to its summer habitat in early May.

During the summer, a few Kirtland's warblers may range to Wisconsin, Minnesota, and even Ontario or Quebec, Canada. However, they do not nest in these areas.

The population of Kirtland's warblers is increasing. Researchers estimated there were around 3,500 individual birds worldwide as of 2012.

History and conservation measures

The first scientific specimen of the Kirtland's warbler was found in the Bahamas in 1841, but researchers did not locate its nesting grounds in Michigan until 1903. These were located near the Au Sable River at the border of Oscoda and Crawford Counties.

Because of its finicky nesting habits, the Kirtland's warbler probably never existed in great numbers. At the beginning of the 20th century, extensive logging in Michigan reduced the bird's already meager habitat. This was worsened by efforts to suppress wildfires. The warbler breeds in stands of jack pines, which appear only in the years after a fire. Without its proper habitat, the warbler has a lesser range—one that has dwindled from about 15,000 acres (6,000 hectares) in the 1950s and 1960s to around 4,450 acres (1,810 hectares), an area of only 7 square miles (18 square kilometers), in the mid-1990s.

The Kirtland's warbler has also been threatened by the brown-headed cowbird. This bird normally inhabits farmland and meadowland. As forests have been cleared in Michigan, it has expanded its range into that of the Kirtland's warbler. The brown-headed cowbird lays its eggs in the nests of other birds, including the warbler. This behavior is called parasitism (pronounced PAIR-uh-suh-tiz-um). When the cowbird nestlings hatch, they are fed by the original nesting birds, who are following their instincts to feed the hatchlings. They do not know the difference between their own and the cowbird nestlings. Their own nestlings often cannot compete with the more aggressive cowbird nestlings for food, and some of them starve to death. From the 1930s to the 1970s, as many as 70 percent of warbler nests were believed to be parasitized by the cowbird.

Conservation efforts in both the Bahamas and Michigan have successfully addressed both of these threats. Better forest management, including cultivation of stands of jack pine, has increased the warbler's range to around 10,000 acres (4,000 hectares). Cowbird trapping and relocation programs have decreased parasitism on the warblers from 70 percent to 3 percent.

As a result of these steps, the Kirtland's warbler population quadrupled between the mid-1990s and 2012, and its numbers are still increasing. Based on the improving outlook for the species, the International Union for Conservation of Nature and Natural Resources (IUCN) changed the warbler's status from vulnerable to near threatened in 2005.

Woodpecker, red-cockaded
Picoides borealis (also *Leuconotopicus borealis*)

PHYLUM: Chordata
CLASS: Aves
ORDER: Piciformes
FAMILY: Picidae
STATUS: Near threatened, IUCN Endangered, ESA
RANGE: USA (Alabama, Arkansas, Florida, Georgia, Louisiana, Mississippi, Missouri, North Carolina, Oklahoma, South Carolina, Texas, Virginia)

Woodpecker, red-cockaded
Picoides borealis (also *Leuconotopicus borealis*)

Description and biology

The red-cockaded woodpecker takes its name from the tiny red patches, or cockades (ribbons used to ornament hats in the 1800s), on the sides of its head. Females lack these patches. An average red-cockaded woodpecker measures 7 inches (18 centimeters) long and has a wingspan of 15 inches (38 centimeters). The plumage (covering of feathers) on the bird's upperparts is black with white stripes. Its chest and belly are white with black-flecked sides. The bird has a black crown and prominent black bands that start at its bill and run down both sides of its neck. On each cheek, between the band and the bird's crown, is a large white patch.

The red-cockaded woodpecker feeds on insects (ants, beetles, caterpillars, and roaches) and spiders both on and under tree bark, particularly on pine trees. It also eats fruits, berries, and seeds. The bird nests in groups called clans. These clans consist of a male-female pair, their

A red-cockaded woodpecker perches on a tree trunk at the Noxubee National Wildlife Refuge in Mississippi. © TIM THOMPSON/ENCYCLOPEDIA/ CORBIS.

Crustaceans

Amphipod, Illinois cave
Gammarus acherondytes

PHYLUM: Arthropoda
CLASS: Malacostraca
ORDER: Amphipoda
FAMILY: Gammaridae
STATUS: Endangered, IUCN
Endangered, ESA
RANGE: USA (Illinois)

Amphipod, Illinois cave
Gammarus acherondytes

Description and biology

The Illinois cave amphipod is a small freshwater crustacean (shellfish). It is light blue-gray in color, with small eyes and one long and one shorter antenna. A male Illinois cave amphipod is usually about 0.8 inches (2 centimeters) long and a female about 0.5 to 0.6 inches (1.3 to 1.5 centimeters) long. Illinois cave amphipods live in utter darkness in cave streams. They need very cold water and avoid light. They cannot leave their caves, so they will eat any kind of food matter they can find by means of their keen sense of touch. Food sources include dead animals, plants, and bacteria.

Illinois cave amphipods are extremely sensitive to pollutants that are introduced into their water supply. The species is an excellent indicator of the quality of the water in the cave systems it inhabits and the groundwater from the surrounding area.

Because the Illinois cave amphipod lives underground and away from humans, little is known about the behavior of this species.

Habitat and current distribution

The Illinois cave amphipod lives in karst regions (areas composed of limestone that feature sinkholes, underground streams, and caverns). It is known to occur only in Monroe and St. Clair Counties in southwestern Illinois.

History and conservation measures

The Illinois cave amphipod is endemic (native to and occurring only in a particular region) to several cave systems in Monroe and St. Clair Counties in southern Illinois. The species was once known to occur in six cave systems, all within a 10-mile (16-kilometer) radius of Waterloo, Illinois. In 1995 the species was found in only three of these systems, all in Monroe County. This reduction in its range signaled a decline in the population of the species. The species was still present in three cave systems by 2001, but little research has been carried out since then because of a lack of funding.

Groundwater contamination, usually from pesticides used by farmers, is the principal threat to the species. Contamination from human and animal wastes from sewers and septic systems and livestock feedlots in the area also pose a grave danger. Scientists believe that the poor water quality, if not corrected, will probably cause the extinction of the species. People sometimes use sinkholes in the karst region inhabited by the amphipods as a place to dump trash and other pollutants. Because there is no natural filter in a sinkhole to stop the pollutants from reaching the underground waters, the risk of contamination is very high. When amphipods are damaged or killed by the contamination of the streams and groundwater, there is good reason to believe that humans who use the same water sources will be affected as well.

The small range of the Illinois cave amphipod is very close to St. Louis, Missouri, and so the habitat may face further harm from the urban environment. The Illinois Department of Natural Resources owns the entrances to two of the three caves known to be Illinois cave amphipod habitats, which means that the state can control access to the caves in order to protect the Illinois cave amphipod. The entrances to the third cave are privately owned but have been designated as nature reserves. A U.S. Fish and Wildlife Service recovery plan written in 2002 set a goal of full recovery for the species by 2023, but the plan has not received enough funding to stay on track. The Illinois cave amphipod is currently protected by the Illinois Endangered Species Protection Act, which prohibits harming or killing it.

Crayfish, Hell Creek Cave
Cambarus zophonastes

PHYLUM: Arthropoda
CLASS: Malacostraca
ORDER: Decapoda
FAMILY: Cambaridae
STATUS: Critically endangered, IUCN
Endangered, ESA
RANGE: USA (Arkansas)

Crayfish, Hell Creek Cave
Cambarus zophonastes

Description and biology

The Hell Creek Cave crayfish is white. It has small eyes that lack any pigment (color) and a spined rostrum (snout). An average adult measures 2.6 inches (6.6 centimeters) long. Like other crayfish, it feeds on both plants and animals, including algae, snails, insects, worms, and mussels.

Although appearing similar to lobsters (their saltwater cousins), crayfish have a different life cycle. They do not pass through any larval stages but go directly from an egg to a miniature adult form. Hell Creek Cave crayfish reproduce very slowly. Biologists (people who study living organisms) believe they lay eggs once every five years, on average. As in other crayfish species, the female Hell Creek Cave crayfish shelters her fertilized eggs by carrying them attached to her abdomen. After the eggs hatch, the young crayfish cling to that spot on the mother's body for several weeks before letting go.

The Hell Creek Cave crayfish reproduce very slowly, possibly due to a lack of nourishment. © DANTE FENOLIO/SCIENCE SOURCE.

Crayfish are preyed on by bass, sunfish, raccoons, otters, herons, and kingfishers.

Habitat and current distribution

Until 2005, the Hell Creek Cave crayfish was only known to exist in a deep pool in Hell Creek Cave, which is located in the Ozark Mountains in Stone County, Arkansas. Surveys conducted in the mid-1980s recorded fewer than 50 crayfish at this site and the population remained near that figure into the early 21st century. In 2005 the crayfish was found for the first time in nearby Nesbitt Spring Cave, also in Stone County. A 2006 survey found a total of 23 crayfish in the two caves.

Hell Creek Cave is mostly wet and muddy throughout the year. Many of its passages are flooded during the rainy seasons and after storms. A narrow, shallow stream leads to the pool inhabited by the crayfish. The pool is approximately 150 feet (46 meters) away from the cave entrance. Nesbitt Spring Cave has similar conditions, and its crayfish

Did You Know?

Crayfish are found on all continents on Earth except Africa and Antarctica. They are an essential part of the food chain. They feed on algae, insects, mussels, and snails, while in turn being fed on by fish, herons, otters, and other larger animals. This feeding balance has been maintained for hundreds of thousands of years. However, as of 2015, a third of the world's nearly 600 crayfish species are under threat of extinction. The reasons for this vary by region. North America is home to the world's greatest diversity of crayfish species, found in abundance in the southeastern United States. These species are threatened by pollution, the expansion of cities, and the damming of rivers. The other hot spot for crayfish is southeastern Australia, where invasive species (species from a different ecosystem that spread or multiply and cause harm when they are introduced into a new environment), agriculture, climate change, and harvesting of crayfish are threatening the many species of freshwater crayfish found there.

were found in a pool about 200 feet (61 meters) from the entrance.

History and conservation measures

There are about 330 known species of crayfish, which are also known as crawfish or crawdads. Although many of these species are under review for inclusion on the U.S. Endangered Species List, the Hell Creek Cave crayfish, added in 1987, was one of the first crayfish placed on the list.

This species of crayfish faces a number of threats. A surface stream supplies water to Hell Creek Cave's pool. This stream can easily become polluted with wastes from nearby industries. Once polluted, the stream will in turn contaminate the pool, destroying the crayfish's fragile habitat. Septic system leaks, hazardous chemical spills on highways, and runoff (water that drains away, bringing substances with it) from poultry farms are potential dangers at the Nesbitt Spring Cave location.

Biologists believe the Hell Creek Cave crayfish reproduces so slowly because it does not get enough nourishment. Hell Creek Cave has a shortage of organic matter for the crayfish to use as energy. In the past, most of this organic matter came from the guano (feces) of gray bats (*Myotis grisescens*). However, the gray bat is now an endangered species. It has disappeared from Hell Creek Cave as well as from many other caves.

A tract of land that includes the entrance to Hell Creek Cave is under protection and a gate has been installed on the entrance to the cave. This act should limit the number of humans entering the cave and disturbing its ecosystem (an ecological system including all of its living things and their environment). Nesbitt Spring Cave is located on private property and does not have a gate, but the property owners are committed to protecting the cave and its environment.

Isopod, Madison Cave
Antrolana lira

PHYLUM: Arthropoda
CLASS: Malacostraca
ORDER: Isopoda
FAMILY: Cirolanidae
STATUS: Vulnerable, IUCN
Threatened, ESA
RANGE: USA (Virginia, West Virginia)

Isopod, Madison Cave
Antrolana lira

Description and biology

Isopods are tiny, shrimplike crustaceans (shellfish) that have flattened bodies and no carapace (pronounced CARE-a-pace) or shell. The Madison Cave isopod measures up to 0.7 inches (1.8 centimeters) long and 0.16 inches (0.41 centimeters) wide. Although it has no eyes, it has a pair of short antennae and a pair of long antennae. It is colorless and has seven pairs of long legs. Its diet consists of decaying organic matter, such as leaf litter (dead leaves), small twigs, wood particles, and insect remains.

Biologists (people who study living organisms) have been unable to observe the reproductive habits of this isopod.

Habitat and current distribution

The Madison Cave isopod is found only in deep caves and fissures (long narrow cracks or openings) in the Shenandoah Valley, from Lexington,

The Madison Cave isopod is found in the flooded caves of Virginia and West Virginia. © LYNDA RICHARDSON/DOCUMENTARY VALUE/CORBIS.

Virginia, to Harpers Ferry, West Virginia. Madison Cave isopods prefer to inhabit freshwater pools that have clay banks.

History and conservation measures

The first Madison Cave isopod specimen was not collected until 1958. In 1964 biologists named the species after the cave where it was first found, although they now know that it exists in other caves as well. Madison Cave has a significant place in U.S. history. Thomas Jefferson (1743–1826), a U.S. founding father, mapped the cave, the first instance of cave mapping in the United States. First U.S. president George Washington's (1732–1799) signature also appears on one of the walls in the cave. The Madison Cave isopod is the only species of its kind found in North America north of Texas.

The isopod faces a number of threats, especially contamination of underground water and loss of its habitat. Cave pools can become quickly contaminated with pollution when nearby surface water that feeds the caves becomes polluted. Conservationists (people who work to manage and protect nature) worry that herbicides and insecticides, which run off into rivers from nearby farms, could easily reach toxic (poisonous) levels in some of these caves.

The isopod's habitat has also been damaged by humans. Many people like to explore caves (an activity called spelunking) for recreation. Others have entered caves in the past to collect bat guano or feces, which is used to produce saltpeter (potassium nitrate), a component of gunpowder. As people have walked along the banks of cave pools, they have knocked clay into the pools, destroying the isopod's habitat by increasing the amount of silt (mineral particles) in the water.

In 1981 a gate was put up over the entrance to Madison Cave. Only scientists and educators seeking to study the Madison Cave isopod and other species in its habitat are now allowed access to the cave. Biologists have worked successfully with people who live near other caves in the isopod's habitat to decrease the human impact on the species and reduce contamination. Protecting the species also protects people, because reducing pollutants makes groundwater cleaner and safer for drinking.

Shrimp, California freshwater
Syncaris pacifica

PHYLUM: Arthropoda
CLASS: Malacostraca
ORDER: Decapoda
FAMILY: Atyidae
STATUS: Endangered, IUCN
Endangered, ESA
RANGE: USA (California)

Shrimp, California freshwater
Syncaris pacifica

Description and biology

The California freshwater shrimp is similar in appearance to the common marine (ocean) shrimp. It has a greenish-gray body with light-blue tail fins. When seen in the water, it looks transparent. Females can measure up to 1.8 inches (4.6 centimeters) in length, while males are from 1.2 to 1.5 inches (3 to 3.8 centimeters) long.

After mating, a female California freshwater shrimp carries her eggs on her body throughout the winter. The eggs, which number between 50 and 120, grow very slowly over a 9-month period. Only about half of the eggs hatch.

Habitat and current distribution

This species of shrimp is found only in 12 areas of three California counties: Napa, Marin, and Sonoma. Biologists (people who study living organisms) do not know the total number of these shrimp currently in existence.

The California freshwater shrimp prefers to inhabit quiet, clear freshwater streams in low elevations of up to 410 feet (125 meters). These streams are usually tree lined and have underwater vegetation (plant life) and exposed tree roots. Water in the streams is fairly slow moving.

History and conservation measures

The range of the California freshwater shrimp has not changed, but the areas within that range where the shrimp is found have decreased. The shrimp has disappeared completely from some streams that it formerly inhabited.

The primary threat to this shrimp is the loss or destruction of its habitat. Many streams in its range have been diverted or dammed to help irrigate farms. In some areas, the water quality of the streams has decreased. Runoff (water that drains away, bringing substances with it) from farms has introduced pesticides and other agricultural chemicals into the water system. The amount of silt (mineral particles) in the water has also increased because of construction along the banks of many streams.

Some dams have been removed in an attempt to restore the California freshwater shrimp's habitat. To further aid in this species' recovery, conservationists (people who work to manage and protect nature) believe that the effects of future damming and construction projects have to be examined.

A recovery plan for the California freshwater shrimp was developed by the U.S. Fish and Wildlife Service in 1998. Its goals are to increase the numbers of California freshwater shrimp so that it is no longer endangered and to improve the habitat for both the species and other organisms that make up its ecosystem (an ecological system including all of its living things and their environment).

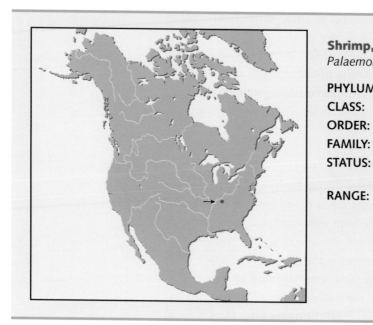

Shrimp, Kentucky cave
Palaemonias ganteri

PHYLUM: Arthropoda
CLASS: Malacostraca
ORDER: Decapoda
FAMILY: Atyidae
STATUS: Vulnerable, IUCN
Endangered, ESA
RANGE: USA (Kentucky)

Shrimp, Kentucky cave
Palaemonias ganteri

Description and biology

The Kentucky cave shrimp is a small freshwater shrimp that grows to a maximum length of only 1.2 inches (3 centimeters). It lacks pigmentation (coloring) and is almost transparent. Because it lives in dark underground streams, it is blind, with undeveloped eyestalks. On its head are two long antennae, as well as a pair of shorter antennae, called antennules, which it uses to sense its surroundings. Its pincers (claws) are of unequal size, and are covered with bristlelike hair. The shrimp molts, or sheds its exoskeleton (hard outer covering) every 40 to 50 days.

The Kentucky cave shrimp spends most of its time on the bottom of streams, using its 10 walking legs to crawl across the bottom in search of organic matter, such as decaying plants, bat feces, algae, fungi, and insect remains. The shrimp is an important part of the ecosystem (an ecological system including all of its living things and their environment) of the cave, since it eats the decaying matter in the cave. It is also a food source for other animals, such as fish, that eat the shrimp for nourishment.

Female cave shrimp carry up to 33 eggs at a time; eggs usually hatch in late summer or fall. The tiny hatchlings are able to swim off on their own immediately; their parents do not care for them.

Habitat and current distribution

The Kentucky cave shrimp lives in nine underground basins in four counties in Kentucky. It prefers large, slow-flowing underground streams that contain a lot of organic matter. At least one location in 2010 was found to have 10,000 individuals; others have as few as 50. Scientists are uncertain whether the population of cave shrimp is currently stable, growing, or decreasing.

History and conservation measures

Pollution is the main threat to the Kentucky cave shrimp. The food supply on which it depends is washed into its cave habitat by a complex system of sinkholes and streams. Fertilizers, insecticides, and herbicides are used on the surface near the caves. These chemicals run off into the waterways supplying the caves. Once this water becomes contaminated, so does the shrimp's food supply and habitat.

Another potential threat is the possibility of inbreeding (animals mating with relatives) in the basins with very low Kentucky cave shrimp populations. Inbreeding, in turn, results in a lower genetic diversity (variety of biological units that pass on inherited traits) because there are fewer individuals whose genes are being passed on. This can cause genetic disease and poor health in subsequent generations.

Three of the Kentucky cave shrimp's underground basins are protected because they are within Mammoth Cave National Park; another three systems are partially in the park. The International Union for Conservation of Nature and Natural Resources (IUCN) continues to list the species as vulnerable because of its limited range and fragmented (broken into smaller areas that no longer border each other) habitat.

Tadpole shrimp, vernal pool
Lepidurus packardi

PHYLUM: Arthropoda
CLASS: Branchiopoda
ORDER: Notostraca
FAMILY: Triopsidae
STATUS: Endangered, IUCN
Endangered, ESA
RANGE: USA (California)

Tadpole shrimp, vernal pool
Lepidurus packardi

Description and biology

The adult vernal pool tadpole shrimp is 0.6 to 3.3 inches (1.5 to 8.4 centimeters) in length. It has a carapace (pronounced CARE-a-pace), or shieldlike shell, attached to its head region. Two fused (grown together) eyes are on top of the carapace. The covering stretches down over the tadpole shrimp's 30 to 35 pairs of legs. These legs are called phyllopods (FILL-uh-pods) and are used for swimming. They also function as gills, taking oxygen from the water into the shrimp's body.

The tadpole shrimp's abdomen pokes out beyond the carapace. Attached to the abdomen are two thin, long tails, with a paddlelike fin between them. Vernal pool tadpole shrimp are light to dark green with brown spots or smears, or brown with green spots or smears. In muddy water, the species can appear translucent or semitransparent.

Vernal pools are temporary pools of water created by seasonal snowmelt or rainfall. The vernal pool tadpole shrimp is named because it lives

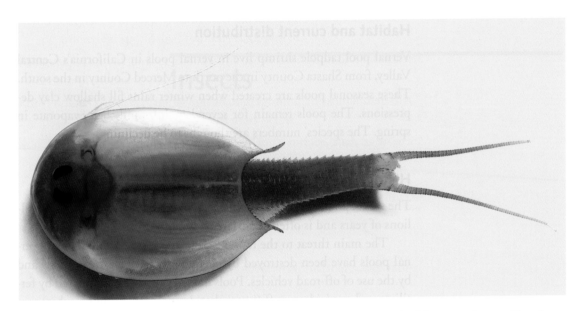

Tadpole shrimp, an ancient species found in vernal (temporary) freshwater pools in central California, are threatened by urban development and agricultural activity in the region. © ALAN HILLS/DK IMAGES.

in these pools. The tadpole shrimp grows to adulthood in 25 days and reproduces just 54 days after it is born. It is believed that each tadpole shrimp has both male and female reproductive organs. This may mean they can reproduce on their own or that any individual can mate with any other individual. These adaptations are important because the pools where tadpole shrimp live are short lived. Thus, the species has little time to find a mate and reproduce.

Tadpole shrimp lay up to 6 clutches (eggs produced at one time) of between 32 and 61 eggs, called cysts, during the winter wet season. The cysts are placed on the bottom of the pools and are very resistant to drought and heat. When the pool dries up, the eggs remain. They can last for up to 10 years. The next time the pool fills up, the eggs will hatch, and the cycle begins again.

Vernal pool tadpole shrimp have a wide-ranging diet, eating other small invertebrates (animals with no backbone), amphibian eggs, plants, and decaying material.

The vernal pool tadpole shrimp should not be confused with *Triops longicaudatus*, a North American freshwater shrimp often called the longtail tadpole shrimp or the American tadpole shrimp.

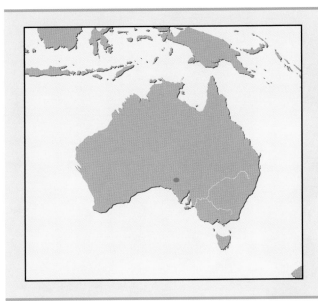

Ant, Australian
Nothomyrmecia macrops

PHYLUM: Arthropoda
CLASS: Insecta
ORDER: Hymenoptera
FAMILY: Formicidae
STATUS: Critically endangered, IUCN
RANGE: Australia

Ant, Australian
Nothomyrmecia macrops

Description and biology

Biologists (people who study living organisms) have identified about 9,500 species of ants (the actual number of ant species on Earth may be two or three times that many). The Australian ant, also known as the dinosaur ant, is considered one of the most primitive ants alive. Ants evolved from wasps, and the Australian ant is the most wasplike ant known. Workers measure approximately 0.4 inches (1 centimeter) long and are golden yellow. They have long jaws and a single waist node (narrow area where the abdomen attaches to the thorax or chest). Their stings are very strong and effective. These ants have a sound-producing organ on their abdomens that they use to create a barely audible chirp. In related ant species, this organ is located on the back.

Australian ants emerge from their nests shortly after nightfall to forage for insects. They do not return to their nests until just before dawn. Biologists believe most ant species use scent markers to navigate. As they

The Australian ant is sensitive to disruptions in its habitat. © MARK MOFFETT/MINDEN PICTURES/CORBIS.

travel above ground, ants lay down a chemical from a gland located at the tip of their abdomen. After they have collected enough food, the ants return to their nests by following these odor trails.

An ant colony is an all-female society. Queens are winged females who produce young. Workers, soldiers, and other specialized members of a colony are all wingless, infertile females (these are the ones normally seen traveling above ground). The only function of winged males is to impregnate or fertilize virgin queens. Once they have done so, these males die. Once a queen has mated with numerous males, she stores the sperm and returns to the nest. She then lays her eggs. Those eggs that are fertilized with the sperm develop into females. Unfertilized eggs develop into males. Females become queens or workers depending on the type of food they are fed during their larval (immature) stage.

In Australian ant colonies, virgin queens and males are produced in late spring and early autumn. Although biologists have not witnessed mating activity, they believe the queens and the males leave their colonies in late summer to mate in flight. Australian ant colonies are relatively small, including between 30 and 100 individuals.

Habitat and current distribution

Australian ants are found only in the Australian state of South Australia. They occupy several sites in an area measuring less than 0.4 square miles (1 square kilometer). Their total population number is unknown.

These ants prefer to inhabit woodlands dominated by tall eucalyptus trees. The ground in these areas is covered with a thin layer of leaf debris. Few herbs or grasses grow there. Nests are located underground and have concealed entrances.

History and conservation measures

Biologists originally believed this ant species had inhabited only Western Australia. However, after its initial discovery in 1934, no further evidence of this species could be found in that region. In 1977 a site was discovered in South Australia, but it was destroyed shortly afterward when workers laid an underground telephone line in the area. Since then, three other sites have been discovered nearby.

Habitat destruction is the major threat to this ant. Human populations are increasing in the Australian ant's limited range. Since the ants forage (search for food) in trees, bush fires are also a serious danger; a fire at night could kill 50 percent of a colony's workers, effectively destroying the colony.

Australian ants only emerge from their colony when temperatures are cool, perhaps to avoid other ant species that prey on them. Global warming and warmer temperatures could prevent Australian ants from foraging, causing the ants to starve. Measures to reduce global warming are essential if the Australian ant is to survive.

In 2002 the Australian ant was turned down for protection under the Environment Protection and Biodiversity Conservation Act of Australia based on a lack of scientific information on the species. The International Union for Conservation of Nature and Natural Resources (IUCN), however, listed the species as critically endangered beginning in 1996.

Beetle, American burying
Nicrophorus americanus

PHYLUM: Arthropoda
CLASS: Insecta
ORDER: Coleoptera
FAMILY: Silphidae
STATUS: Critically endangered, IUCN
Endangered, ESA
RANGE: USA (Arkansas, Kansas,
Massachusetts, Missouri, Nebraska,
Ohio, Oklahoma, Rhode Island, South
Dakota, Texas)

Beetle, American burying
Nicrophorus americanus

Description and biology

The American burying beetle, also known as the giant carrion beetle, is the largest of the North American carrion beetles (those that feed on carrion, or the decaying flesh of dead animals). This shiny black beetle reaches an average length of 1 to 1.4 inches (2.5 to 3.5 centimeters). It has bright orange or red spots on the plate covering its head, on the plate immediately behind, and on the plates covering its forewings.

These beetles often fight over carrion. Males fight males, and females fight females. When one male and one female remain, they form a couple. Working together, they dig out the soil beneath the carcass (dead body) until it is completely buried about 8 inches (20 centimeters) deep.

In the underground chamber, the beetles coat the carcass with secretions from their mouths and anuses. These secretions strip away the

The American burying beetle, which was once prevalent in the United States and Canada, has seen its population drop due to changes to its habitat and food supply. © MARK MOFFETT/MINDEN PICTURES/CORBIS.

carcass's fur or feathers while preserving what remains. In a passageway near the carcass, the female lays her eggs, and they hatch in a few days. The parents then feed the larvae (young) from the decomposing carcass for about 50 days, until the larvae develop into adults.

This complex parental teamwork—both in preparing the carcass and in raising the young—makes the American burying beetle unique among beetle species.

Habitat and current distribution

These beetles inhabit grasslands, pastures, shrub thickets, and oak-hickory forests.

The American burying beetle is currently found in 84 counties within the United States. These counties are in Arkansas, Kansas, Massachusetts, Missouri, Nebraska, Ohio, Oklahoma, Rhode Island, South Dakota, and Texas. The populations in Massachusetts, Missouri, and Ohio were originally bred in captivity and introduced into the wild. The total population size is unknown.

History and conservation measures

The American burying beetle had a range that once extended throughout the eastern and midwestern United States and eastern Canada. Its population, however, has been declining since the 1920s. The beetle has disappeared from more than 90 percent of its former range.

The American burying beetle's numbers have likely declined for a variety of reasons, including habitat loss. When land where this species lives is converted to farmland or grazing land, the change favors mammals and birds that compete with the beetle for carrion. Another reason is that the species depends on carrion of a certain size, such as passenger pigeons. But these birds became extinct immediately before the numbers of American burying beetle began to decline.

When the beetle was listed as an endangered species in 1989, only two populations were known, in Rhode Island and Oklahoma. Since then, American burying beetles have been discovered in Arkansas, Nebraska, Kansas, Texas, and South Dakota. In Massachusetts, Ohio, and Missouri, biologists (people who study living organisms) have bred the beetles in captivity and reintroduced them into the wild. As of 2014, the Missouri population was breeding and thriving, although Massachusetts and Ohio beetle populations have been less successful.

Some conservationists (people who work to manage and protect nature) are concerned about the possible effect of a proposed extension of an oil pipeline on the American burying beetle. Construction of part of the Keystone XL pipeline extension would run from Hardisty in Alberta, Canada, through parts of Montana, South Dakota, and Nebraska. Environmentalists fear that it will kill beetles and destroy their habitat. However, the U.S. government believes that the pipeline will not cause serious damage to the species.

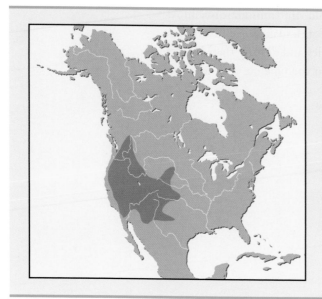

Bumblebee, Morrison
Bombus morrisoni

PHYLUM: Arthropoda
CLASS: Insecta
ORDER: Hymenoptera
FAMILY: Apidae
STATUS: Vulnerable, IUCN
RANGE: Canada, USA (Arizona, California, Colorado, Idaho, Kansas, Nevada, New Mexico, Oklahoma, Oregon, South Dakota, Texas, Utah, Washington, Wyoming)

Bumblebee, Morrison
Bombus morrisoni

Description and biology

The Morrison bumblebee is a mountain and desert species that mostly lives in open, dry scrub (land covered with stunted trees and shrubs). It nests underground, in buildings or in tufts of grass.

Like most bees, the Morrison bumblebee is a social insect that lives in colonies. These colonies consist of an egg-laying queen, nonmating workers, and mating males and new queens. In the winter, all colony members die except for the queens, which go into hibernation. In the early spring, the queens emerge, forage for pollen, and look for a new nest site. When the workers are born, they help with foraging and building the nest.

Female bumblebees can sting repeatedly if disturbed, although if left alone they will generally ignore humans. Bumblebees feed on pollen and the nectar of flowering plants. Morrison bumblebees feed particularly on the following plants: *Asclepias, Astragalus, Chrysothamnus,*

The Morrison bumblebee, native to the western region of Canada and the United States, is threatened by pesticide use and disease.
© MICHAEL DURHAM/MINDEN PICTURES/CORBIS.

Cirsium, Cleome, Ericameria, Helianthus, Melilotus, and *Senecio.* Bumblebees are adapted to different plants partly on the basis of the length of their tongues. The Morrison bumblebee is short-tongued.

Like other bumblebees, the Morrison bumblebee is yellow and black. Queens are 0.87 to 1.02 inches (2.2 to 2.6 centimeters) long; workers are 0.47 to 0.87 inches (1.2 to 2.2 centimeters) long. They have short, even hairs and short heads. Males are 0.58 to 0.77 inches (1.5 to 2 centimeters) long and have enlarged eyes. The males engage in perching behavior and will chase moving objects when seeking a mate.

Habitat and current distribution

The Morrison bumblebee is found in the mountainous region of western North America, including California in the United States and British Columbia in Canada. It also lives in the desert, east as far as New

Mexico and Texas and north as far as South Dakota. It is found in the western part of some midwestern states. It has been found in Arizona, California, Colorado, Idaho, Kansas, Nevada, New Mexico, Oklahoma, Oregon, South Dakota, Texas, Utah, Washington, and Wyoming.

History and conservation measures

The Morrison bumblebee was once quite common throughout its range. It has suffered a serious decline, however, with its numbers dropping by about 57 percent between roughly 2004 and 2014. It continues to thrive in parts of Utah, however, and it is the most common *Bombus* species at Grand Staircase–Escalante National Monument in that state.

The exact threats facing the Morrison bumblebee are uncertain. There has been much high-profile discussion of massive honeybee die-offs, but bumblebee species are also diminishing across the world. In North America, such species as the western bumblebee (*Bombus occidentalis*), the rusty-patched bumblebee (*Bombus affinis*), and the yellow-banded bumblebee (*Bombus terricola*) have seen their numbers drop by as much as 95 percent. Scientists suspect that climate change and pesticides may be factors. Fungal infections have also killed many bees, perhaps because they were weakened by other threats.

The danger is not just to bees, however. Bumblebees are efficient pollinators, and they are vital to growing crops. At least 80 percent of the world's food crops are pollinated by bumblebees and other wild pollinators, while honeybees are responsible for pollinating only 15 percent of crops. Bumblebees are also ecologically important in the wild, where they pollinate numerous plants and flowers. The loss of the Morrison and other bumblebee species could therefore have major financial and environmental consequences.

As of 2015 the U.S. Fish and Wildlife Service (USFWS) had yet to list any bee species on the Endangered Species List. Such action would provide legal protection for species such as the Morrison bumblebee. However, in 2014 the USFWS announced that it would take measures to improve the habitat of bees and other pollinators by phasing out the use of neonicotinoids (a type of pesticide linked to declines in bee populations) in all U.S. wildlife refuge areas.

Butterfly, bay checkerspot
Euphydryas editha bayensis

PHYLUM: Arthropoda
CLASS: Insecta
ORDER: Lepidoptera
FAMILY: Nymphalidae
STATUS: Threatened, ESA
RANGE: USA (California)

Butterfly, bay checkerspot
Euphydryas editha bayensis

Description and biology

The bay checkerspot butterfly is a medium-sized butterfly with a maximum wingspan of 2.25 inches (5.72 centimeters). Females are slightly larger than males. The butterfly's black upper surface is checkered with bright red, white, and yellow markings. Its yellow underside has sharp black and red patterns.

The life cycle of a bay checkerspot butterfly takes about a year to complete. The insect undergoes four stages: egg, larva, pupa (cocoon), and adult. This four-stage cycle is referred to as a complete metamorphosis (pronounced met-uh-MORE-fuh-sis) or change.

After mating in early spring, females lay eggs on host plants in batches of 20 to 95. Some females lay as many as 1,200 eggs in a season, but the normal range is 600 to 700. The eggs soon hatch and the larvae or caterpillars begin feeding on their host plants. By late summer,

The bay checkerspot butterfly is native to California. © PURE-STOCK/ALAMY.

if the larvae have developed enough or if the plants have begun to dry up from the summer heat, the larvae enter a dormant or resting stage. When winter rains revive the dry plants, the larvae become active again. In late winter, they enter the pupal, or cocoon, stage, transforming in two weeks into adult bay checkerspot butterflies. The adults feed on the nectar of several plants.

Habitat and current distribution

Bay checkerspot butterflies are known to exist only in San Mateo and Santa Clara Counties in California. Biologists (people who study living organisms) believe that there are only four or five core populations of the species. Because the number of butterflies alive each year changes dramatically, the total population size has never been estimated.

This butterfly inhabits grasslands where dwarf plantain and owl's clover—the butterfly larva's host plants—grow in high numbers.

History and conservation measures

Bay checkerspot butterflies once inhabited numerous areas around the San Francisco Bay, including the San Francisco Peninsula, the mountains near San Jose, the Oakland hills, and several spots in Alameda County. All of these habitat areas were lost as urban development exploded in the region in the 20th century. The butterflies are currently threatened with the loss of their host plants to animal grazing, brush fires, and introduced grassland plants.

In Santa Clara County, much of the remaining butterfly habitat is on property owned by a landfill corporation. An agreement between the corporation, the San Jose city government, and conservationists (people who work to manage and protect nature) established a butterfly preserve on the property. The landfill company also provides thousands of larvae for relocation to other sites in Santa Clara and San Mateo Counties.

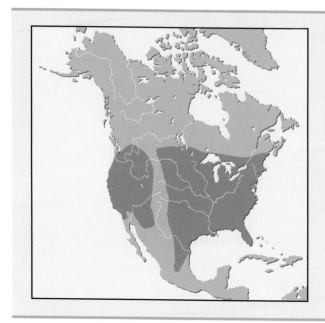

Butterfly, monarch
Danaus plexippus plexippus

PHYLUM: Arthropoda
CLASS: Insecta
ORDER: Lepidoptera
FAMILY: Nymphalidae
STATUS: Under review by U.S. Fish and Wildlife Service as a possible endangered species
RANGE: Canada, Mexico, United States

Butterfly, monarch
Danaus plexippus plexippus

Description and biology

The colorful monarch butterfly, sometimes called the "king of butterflies," sports reddish-orange wings with black veins. The margins (edges) of the wings are black with a series of small white spots. The forewings (front wings) have several orange spots near the wingtip. Underneath, the white spots are larger and the wingtips are yellow brown. Males have a black spot of specialized scales in the center of their hindwing (back wing) and narrower veins; they are slightly larger than females. The butterfly's body is black. Its wingspan is 3.5 to 4 inches (8.9 to 10.2 centimeters) wide. There are six subspecies of monarch butterfly. One of them, *Danaus plexippus plexippus*, is under review as a potential endangered species by the U.S. Fish and Wildlife Service (USFWS).

Monarch butterfly larvae feed only on the leaves and flowers of milkweed plants. Adults feed on nectar from many plants, including

The monarch butterfly has experienced a dramatic drop in population since the 1990s as farmers have increased their use of pesticides that kill milkweed, which is the larval monarch's only source of food. © SARI ONEAL/SHUTTERSTOCK.COM.

alfalfa, goldenrod, lilac, and milkweed. The butterfly's bright colors and contrasting patterns discourage predators. Their bodies store substances from the milkweed that make them unappealing to most predators.

Monarchs are migratory. The route of the *Danaus plexippus plexippus* subspecies is through the United States, and they are the most frequently seen butterflies in the country. In early spring, a new generation of butterflies is born in northern Mexico or the southeastern United States. These butterflies fly north at a rate of 25 to 30 miles (40 to 48 kilometers) a day. They have a life span of five to eight weeks, during which time they mate, lay eggs, and die. Two or three more generations follow the same pattern, traveling northward. By summer's end, butterflies reach the northern United States or southern Canada.

The next generation lives six to eight months and undertakes a southward migration of 2,000 to 3,000 miles (3,200 to 4,800 kilometers). Most monarchs east of the Rocky Mountains migrate in the millions to Mexico. Those west of the Rocky Mountains fly to sites on California's central-southern coast. Then, in February and March, they mate and fly north. They soon die, the first generation of the year hatches, and the cycle begins again. A small population lives in Florida and other locations in the southernmost United States and does not migrate.

Habitat and current distribution

The monarch butterfly lives wherever milkweed plants occur: fields, meadows, marshes, roadsides, cities, and suburbs. The *Danaus plexippus plexippus* subspecies is found in southern Canada, the entire United States, and Mexico. Small nonnative populations of this subspecies occur worldwide. In 2015, some 56 million monarchs wintered in Mexico.

History and conservation measures

Long before Europeans arrived in Mexico, people living near monarchs' winter sites celebrated their yearly arrival, believing that they carry the souls of long-gone ancestors. In the United States, seven states have named this butterfly their state insect. In the mid-1990s scientists counted 1 billion monarchs, but since then, the population has declined by more than 90 percent. The main reason for this is the increasing agricultural use of glyphosate, an herbicide (plant poison) that kills milkweed in croplands. Other threats to the monarch butterfly include illegal logging at Mexican sites where monarch butterflies spend the winter; new real estate developments that clear land for homes in the United States; and heat waves and severe storms associated with climate change.

The U.S. government is considering granting endangered species status to the monarch butterfly and is scheduled to reach a decision in 2016. Meanwhile, the government has committed about $5 million to conservation projects such as planting milkweed. Conservation groups have asked the government to reevaluate the use of glyphosate. In addition, conservation organizations in Mexico, the United States, and Canada have requested that the UNESCO World Heritage Committee (an organization of the United Nations) include the monarch winter site in Mexico on its List of World Heritage in Danger. Listed sites receive conservation funds and attract worldwide attention. Many environmental groups offer ideas on how people can work to help save the monarch. The USFWS also began a "Save the Monarch Butterfly" campaign to raise awareness.

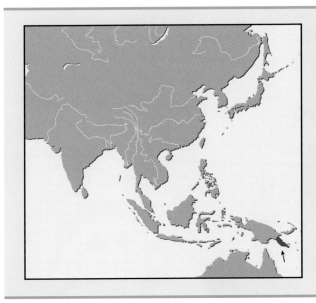

Butterfly, Queen Alexandra's birdwing
Ornithoptera alexandrae (also *Troides alexandrae*)

PHYLUM: Arthropoda
CLASS: Insecta
ORDER: Lepidoptera
FAMILY: Papilionidae
STATUS: Endangered, IUCN
Endangered, ESA
RANGE: Papua New Guinea

Butterfly, Queen Alexandra's birdwing

Ornithoptera alexandrae (also *Troides alexandrae*)

Description and biology

Many biologists (people who study living organisms) believe that the Queen Alexandra's birdwing butterfly is the world's largest butterfly. It has an average head and body length of 3 inches (7.6 centimeters). Females of the species have wingspans measuring more than 10 inches (25.4 centimeters). Males, which are smaller, have wingspans of about 7 inches (17.8 centimeters). Females and males also differ in color. In females, the upper surfaces of the wings have cream markings on a dark, chocolate-brown background. In males, the upper surfaces have iridescent yellow, pale blue, and pale green markings on a black background. In both sexes, the abdomen is yellow, and the lower surface of the wings, where they attach to the butterfly's body, are bright red.

The Queen Alexandra's birdwing butterfly has a seven-month life span. Females lay large eggs, which measure about 0.16 inches

The Queen Alexandra's birdwing butterfly is native to Papua New Guinea. © DEEPU SG/ALAMY.

(0.41 centimeters) in diameter, on the leaves of a particular vine that is poisonous to animals that might eat the butterfly's eggs. The eggs hatch in 11 to 13 days, and the larvae or caterpillars emerge to begin feeding on these leaves. The caterpillars exist for four months before entering the pupal, or cocoon, stage to transform into an adult butterfly. After it has metamorphosed (pronounced met-uh-MORE-fozed) or changed into an adult, the butterfly may live for another three months.

The adult butterfly has few predators, but its eggs are often eaten by ants. Caterpillars are preyed on by snakes, lizards, toads, and birds such as cuckoos and crow pheasants.

Habitat and current distribution

This butterfly species is found in a few sites in Papua New Guinea, mainly on the Popondetta Plain in the northern part of the island. The vine where the butterfly breeds can grow up to 131 feet (40 meters) in length and is found around the crowns of trees. Because the Queen Alexandra's birdwing butterfly flies high and is rarely seen, biologists have been unable to determine any population totals.

Queen Alexandra's birdwing butterflies inhabit primary and secondary lowland rain forests at elevations up to 2,950 feet (900 meters). Biologists have reported seeing male butterflies swarm around large Kwila trees when they are bearing flowers. Those males that do not visit these flowers are not accepted by females to mate. Biologists cannot explain the reason for this.

Did You Know?

The 1951 eruption of Mount Lamington in Oro Province was the worst natural disaster ever to hit Papua New Guinea at that time. More than 2,940 people were killed by lava flows. The volcano was active for six days before it finally erupted, covering most of Oro Province in ash. At the conclusion of the eruption, a dome of lava grew 1,840 feet (560 meters) above the crater before it collapsed. Lava continued to flow out of the crater like toothpaste being squeezed from a tube, forming domes and then collapsing, until 1956. Some biologists believe the volcano's destruction of a large amount of prime habitat was the beginning of the decline of the Queen Alexandra's birdwing butterfly.

History and conservation measures

The Queen Alexandra's birdwing butterfly was identified in 1906, when a female specimen was first collected. During the 20th century the butterfly's habitat was broken up by logging operations and farming. In 1951 the Mount Lamington volcano erupted, destroying about 100 square miles (259 square kilometers) of prime Queen Alexandra's birdwing butterfly habitat.

Large tracts of this butterfly's habitat in the Popondetta region have been converted into cocoa, coffee, rubber, and oil palm plantations. Almost none of the rain forest and the vines that the Queen Alexandra's birdwing butterfly needs to survive still exist. Growing human populations in the region pose a further threat as forests are cleared to create urban areas.

The Queen Alexandra's birdwing butterfly is protected by international treaties, but illegal capture remains a threat. Collectors around the world will pay large amounts of money to own a specimen of the world's largest butterfly. One specimen could cost up to $10,000 on the illegal market.

The Papua New Guinea government has passed legislation safeguarding this and other butterfly species on the island. These laws are strictly enforced. A wildlife management area, including grassland and forest, has been established north of the Popondetta region.

Dragonfly, Hine's emerald
Somatochlora hineana

PHYLUM: Arthropoda
CLASS: Insecta
ORDER: Odonata
FAMILY: Corduliidae
STATUS: Near threatened, IUCN
Endangered, ESA
RANGE: USA (Illinois, Michigan, Missouri, Wisconsin)

Dragonfly, Hine's emerald
Somatochlora hineana

Description and biology

The Hine's emerald dragonfly is the only dragonfly on the U.S. Endangered Species List. It is a fairly large dragonfly, with a body that is 2.5 inches (6.3 centimeters) long with a wingspan of 3.3 inches (8.4 centimeters). Its bright emerald-green eyes give the insect its name. The body is dark green, and it has two yellow stripes on its thorax (body segment between the head and abdomen).

The life cycle of a dragonfly begins when a female lays more than 500 eggs in shallow water by dipping her body into the water. The following spring, immature dragonflies hatch from the eggs. These remain in the water for two to four years, eating small insects and larvae and molting (shedding their skin) often as they grow. Finally, they leave the water and molt once more, emerging as a flying adult dragonfly. They live for only four to six weeks after becoming an adult. This time is spent in flight, eating other flying insects, then finally mating before they die.

Habitat and current distribution

The Hine's emerald dragonfly inhabits wetlands (areas where there is a lot of water in the soil, such as swamps or tidal flats) fed by groundwater with limestone bedrock underneath, such as marshes and wet meadows. There are probably more than 30,000 individuals of this species, but biologists (people who study living organisms) do not know the total population size. One county in Wisconsin is thought to contain about two-thirds of the estimated population, and Illinois is estimated to have 86 to 313 adults. Small populations exist in Michigan and Missouri as

The Hine's emerald dragonfly requires a highly specific wetland habitat, which makes it vulnerable to industrial development and other human activity. © PAUL SPARKS/SHUTTERSTOCK.COM.

well. It is thought to be extinct in Ohio, Alabama, and Indiana.

History and conservation measures

Dragonflies evolved at least 300 million years ago. Some prehistoric specimens had nearly 2.5-foot (0.76-meter) wingspans. The Hine's emerald dragonfly, first discovered in 1931, was thought to be extinct until its rediscovery in 1988 in Illinois. Because the dragonfly was found in only a few locations at that point, it was listed as endangered by both the U.S. Fish and Wildlife Service and the International Union for Conservation of Nature and Natural Resources (IUCN). Since that time, however, many new populations of this insect have been discovered. The IUCN therefore changed its listing to near threatened in 2007 and has stated it may change it to least concern in the future.

Habitat destruction is the primary cause for the decline of this species. Wetlands throughout the dragonfly's former range were drained to create urban and commercial areas. Now, many of the areas where the species is found are protected. But the dragonfly's habitat still faces threats of contamination by chemicals, such as pesticides and oil spills from petroleum refineries. These chemicals can both contaminate the wetlands where the dragonfly lives and pollute the groundwater flowing into these wetlands. Invasive species (species from a different ecosystem that spread or multiply and cause harm when they are introduced into a new environment), both plant and animal, also pose a threat. Climate change is another possible threat; drought could harm the species by drying up the wetlands.

A program has been started that removes eggs or young larvae of the Hine's emerald dragonfly and raises them in captivity, returning them to the wild when they are adults.

Did You Know?

Dragonflies are ancient insects, dating back some 300 million years, before the beginning of the age of dinosaurs. Other than being smaller, present-day dragonflies do not differ very much from their ancestors. In fact, modern dragonflies are descendants of the very first winged insects, which were unable to flex their wings flat over their backs. Today, dragonflies are found all over the world except in the polar regions. All dragonflies rely on clean sources of freshwater for their habitat, so their presence is an indicator of good water quality. Dragonflies also serve as a natural mosquito control. A single dragonfly can eat hundreds of mosquitoes in one day.

Did You Know?

There are two subspecies of *Rhaphiomidas terminatus*: the El Segundo flower-loving fly and the Delhi Sands flower-loving fly. The El Segundo fly lived in the El Segundo, California, sand dunes ecosystem (an ecological system including all of its living things and their environment). The ecosystem was completely destroyed in the 1960s when the Los Angeles International Airport was built. It was thought that, with the loss of its habitat, the El Segundo flower-loving fly had become extinct. The fly had not been seen since 1965. Then, in 2001, scientists rediscovered a small colony about 20 miles (32 kilometers) from the fly's original habitat, offering new hope for this subspecies. The story of the El Segundo flower-loving fly illustrates the caution that should be taken in labeling a species as extinct, even if there have been no confirmed sightings in decades.

tat is characterized by fine sandy soil, known as Delhi series sands. All known populations of the fly are within an area with a radius of 8 miles (13 kilometers).

History and conservation measures

Before Southern California became so densely populated, the Colton Sand Dune system encompassed about 40 square miles (104 square kilometers) in the Delhi Sands region. It was the largest inland sand dune system in Southern California, and the Delhi Sands flower-loving fly probably occurred throughout the system. In the 19th century citrus and grape farming was introduced to the area, and large areas were cleared of their native plants. In the 20th century urban sprawl (the spreading of houses, shopping centers, and other city facilities through previously undeveloped land) further reduced the habitat of the Delhi Sands flower-loving fly. After widespread construction, the Colton Sand Dune ecosystem (an ecological system including all of its living things and their environment) had virtually been eliminated. At most, about 1,200 acres (485 hectares) of the original habitat remain in the 2010s; about 98 percent of the ecosystem is gone. All of the 11 or 12 populations of the Delhi Sands flower-loving fly live in tiny, fragmented (broken into smaller areas that no longer border each other) pieces of their former habitat, and most of their native plant foods are gone. Estimates of the existing population are in the low hundreds.

In 1993 the Delhi Sands flower-loving fly became the first fly (and the 17th insect) to be listed as endangered under the Endangered Species Act (ESA). The U.S. Fish and Wildlife Service (USFWS) proposed establishing three recovery units within the remaining ecosystem to protect eight of the existing populations. But the fly's habitat is mostly within privately owned lands, and the pressures from developing communities in the area, which want to clear more land for development, have remained very strong. The federal courts, working under ESA, have stopped some urban development, notably an emergency route for a medical center, in order to protect the fly's remaining habitat, but more construction is expected. There has been some political uproar over the idea that a fly's fate should be placed above the pursuits of humans. Conservationists (people who work to manage and protect nature), however, have argued that the loss of the Delhi Sands flower-loving fly is not all that is at stake. The loss of this species, should it come to pass, would signal the loss of an entire unique ecosystem, with all its biodiversity (variety of life-forms).

The USFWS adopted a recovery plan for the species in 1997. As of 2015, the agency has mapped the habitat area, identified landowners willing to assist with conservation, protected the fly's habitat, and started to develop guidelines for monitoring the fly populations and habitat.

Grasshopper, Zayante band-winged
Trimerotropis infantilis

PHYLUM: Arthropoda
CLASS: Insecta
ORDER: Orthoptera
FAMILY: Acrididae
STATUS: Endangered, IUCN
Endangered, ESA
RANGE: USA (California)

Grasshopper, Zayante band-winged

Trimerotropis infantilis

Description and biology

The Zayante band-winged grasshopper is a small brownish-gray grasshopper with blue hind legs. It has dark bands on its front wings, pale yellow hind wings, and bands around its eyes. Males have an average body length of 0.5 to 0.7 inches (13.7 to 17.2 millimeters). Females are larger than males, with body lengths of 0.8 to 0.9 inches (19.7 to 21.6 millimeters).

Adult Zayante band-winged grasshoppers are active between May and October. When this grasshopper is flushed out of a thicket, it has been observed to fly 3 to 7 feet (0.9 to 2.1 meters) into the air. It then lands on bare ground. It is particularly noticeable when it flies because its hind wings are yellow and produce a buzzing sound. Little is known about the life cycle of the species.

When the Zayante band-winged grasshopper is flushed out of a thicket, it has been observed flying some 3 to 7 feet (0.9 to 2.1 meters) into the air.
© JENNIFER CHU KAELIN.

Habitat and current distribution

The Zayante band-winged grasshopper is found only in Santa Cruz County, California, in the Zayante Sandhills. Its habitat is a sand parkland with a combination of chaparral (low thickets of shrubs and small trees) and ponderosa pine forests. Within the Zayante Sandhills, the grasshopper is concentrated on ridges and hills in areas where plant life is sparse and much of the ground is made up of the loose sand called Zayante soils.

History and conservation measures

The Zayante Sandhills' ecosystem (an ecological system including all its living things and their environment) has been severely reduced by human activities, such as sand mining, the construction of homes and commercial properties, and recreation. Although there was once about 6,265 acres (2,535 hectares) of the sand parkland, approximately 40 percent of the area had been lost by 1997, with only about 3,608 acres (1,460 hectares) remaining.

Another threat to the species is the introduction of nonnative plants to the area. Apparently the shade from new species of trees reduces the usable space for the grasshoppers, while other invading plants move into the space the grasshoppers would otherwise inhabit. Pesticides (chemicals used to kill pests) have also damaged the habitat.

Since the Zayante band-winged grasshopper was listed as endangered under the U.S. Endangered Species Act (ESA), restrictions have been placed on sand miners in the area, and the construction of homes and businesses has been minimized. Research is underway to learn more about the habitat needs of the Zayante band-winged grasshopper. In 2001 the U.S. Fish and Wildlife Service (USFWS) designated 10,560 acres (4,275 hectares) of land in Santa Cruz County, California, as critical habitat for this endangered species. Critical habitat is an area that the USFWS deems essential to the conservation of a species; it is based on the physical and biological needs of the species and the space needed for population growth and normal behavior. The designation does not mean that the land will become a reserve or be managed by the government but that the owners will receive education on the conservation of the Zayante band-winged grasshopper. In fact, in 2011 the USFWS made it easier for landowners to build residential structures in the Zayante Sandhills area.

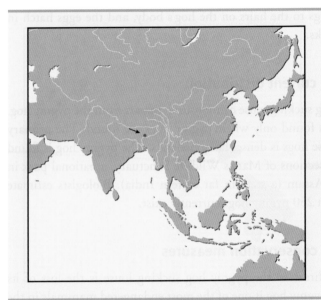

Louse, pygmy hog sucking
Haematopinus oliveri

PHYLUM: Arthropoda
CLASS: Insecta
ORDER: Psocodoea
FAMILY: Haematopinidae
STATUS: Critically endangered, IUCN
RANGE: India

Louse, pygmy hog sucking
Haematopinus oliveri

Description and biology

The pygmy hog sucking louse is a parasite, or an organism that lives on or in another organism (called a host) and gets its nourishment from that host. The louse lives only on the pygmy hog (*Sus salvanius*), the smallest of all pigs and itself a critically endangered species. Because it lives on the hog's body surface, the louse is known as an ectoparasite.

Biologists (people who study living organisms) have not yet been able to collect a male louse specimen. Female pygmy hog sucking lice measure about 0.15 inches (0.38 centimeters) in length. They are wingless and have flat, leathery bodies. Their legs are strong, with powerful claws for clinging to the hairs on the pygmy hog's body. These lice feed only on the hog's blood, and their mouths are specially developed for piercing and sucking.

Biologists do not know exactly how the lice reproduce. Mating seems to take place between males and females on a host hog. Females

One of the primary threats to the Blackburn's sphinx moth is the destruction of its habitat by deer and by feral animals, especially goats. © PHOTO RESOURCE HAWAII/ALAMY.

of an *'aiea*, a native Hawaiian plant that is its preferred host plant. A few days later, the eggs hatch. The male and female die after reproducing. The moths do not live very long; development from the egg stage to a full adult can be as short as 56 days. In its larval (caterpillar) stage, the Blackburn's sphinx moth is a 3.5- to 4-inch (9- to 10-centimeter) caterpillar, almost the size of a hot dog. The caterpillars can be either bright green or gray with white spots or lines. They are usually called "hornworms" because they have a red or black horn on their abdomen. The caterpillars feed on plants from the nightshade family, particularly the *'aiea* plant, from which they eat the leaves, stems, and flowers. However, this plant is becoming rare—three of the four *'aiea* species are listed as endangered. Blackburn's sphinx moths also eat plants that have been introduced to Hawaii, such as a variety of tobacco plants, as well as eggplant and tomato.

After the larval stage, the insect goes through the pupal (cocoon) stage, for which it moves underground. In this stage, it transforms, to eventually rise up to the surface as an adult moth. Adult moths can be found all year but are most often seen between January and April and between September and November.

Habitat and current distribution

The Blackburn's sphinx moth occurs from sea level up to 5,000 feet (1,525 meters) in dry coastal forests. No one knows the number of adult or larval Blackburn's sphinx moths, but it is believed that there are currently four populations on the Hawaiian Islands of Maui, Kaho'olawe, and Hawaii. The main population is in Maui at Kanaio, a natural reserve. This population resides in an area that is both publicly and privately owned. Part of the public area is a natural reserve, while another part of the public area is training ground for the Hawaiian National Guard.

History and conservation measures

At one time the Blackburn's sphinx moth occurred throughout the Hawaiian Islands on Kauai, Oahu, Molokai, Maui, and Hawaii. It was most common in Maui. After the 1940s very few of the species were observed. In the 1970s, after an extensive search for the species failed to turn up any specimens, it was thought to be extinct. Then, in 1984, a population of Blackburn's sphinx moth was discovered at Kanaio. Since then, three other populations have been discovered.

The primary threat to the Blackburn's sphinx moth is the destruction of its habitat by deer and by feral animals (domestic animals that have become wild), particularly goats. The animals eat the native plants and trample their roots and seedlings. The native 'aiea plant, which is important to the moth's survival, is being destroyed rapidly. Because these moths have become so rare, they are valuable in the international market as insect specimens. Humans hunt them for trade. Military maneuvers by the National Guard within the moth's core habitat pose a threat, as do accidental fires in the arid region. Ants and parasitic wasps prey on the eggs and caterpillars.

The Blackburn's sphinx moth was the first Hawaiian insect to be placed on the U.S. Fish and Wildlife Service's (USFWS) Endangered Species List. The USFWS conducts research into the biology, captive breeding, and conservation of the sphinx moth. It also works to restore

The vegetarian wetapungas head out at dusk to feed on the leaves of various shrubs, trees, grasses, and herbs. © LOUISE MURRAY/
SCIENCE SOURCE.

months. Mating and egg laying are usually repeated many times over a period of several days. The male dies soon after the final mating. After laying all of her eggs, sometimes up to 400 in total, the female also dies.

The eggs are approximately 0.27 inches (6.8 millimeters) long and 0.08 inches (2 millimeters) wide. They are laid at a depth of up to 0.78 inches (19.8 millimeters) beneath the soil surface. During midsummer, some of the eggs hatch within three weeks. Most eggs remain undisturbed in the ground through the winter, hatching after 9 or 10 months. The newly hatched wetapungas, called nymphs, are pale, mottled, miniature versions of the adults. During the two years it takes them to reach adulthood, nymphs molt (shed) their skins about 10 times.

Wetapungas are primarily vegetarian (plant-eating). They venture out at dusk to feed on the leaves of a variety of trees, shrubs, herbs, and grasses. They are preyed on by many animals, including cats, rats, pigs, hedgehogs, birds, tuataras, and lizards.

Habitat and current distribution

Wetapungas once inhabited the main New Zealand islands. Their numbers were reduced until they were only present on Little Barrier Island, a small island lying off the northeast coast of North Island, which is among the main New Zealand islands. In the 2010s captive-bred wetapungas were introduced to two other small islands, Tiritiri Matangi Island and Motuora Island (recreation reserves).

Wetapungas are arboreal (living in trees). They spend most of their time in kauri, pohutukawa, kanuka, and other broadleaf trees, seldom coming down to the ground.

History and conservation measures

Before humans began settling on New Zealand's islands, bats were the only warm-blooded mammals in the New Zealand ecosystem (an ecological system including all of its living things and their environment). All species of wetas thrived in safety. Sometime between 1,000 and 2,000 years ago, the Maori (MAU-ree) people from Polynesian islands in the South Pacific first sailed to and settled the New Zealand islands. They brought with them the kiore, or Polynesian rat. It quickly became a predator of wetas.

When European settlers began arriving in the 18th century, they brought to the islands an enormous array of other animals. They cut down the forests for timber and to create farmland, and the whole shape of the New Zealand landscape changed. Those lands that were not cleared were quickly overrun with rodents, deer, goats, pigs, and opossums. In the years since the arrival of European settlers, over 80 percent of New Zealand's natural vegetation (plant life) has disappeared.

All 11 weta species are protected by New Zealand law and their limited habitats have been designated as reserves. However, predators remain in these habitats. Although feral (once domesticated, now wild) cats on Little Barrier Island have been exterminated, the wetapunga is still threatened by the kiore.

In the 2010s captive breeding of the wetapunga proved very successful. Wetapungas were introduced to two other small islands: Tiritiri

Fanshell
Cyprogenia stegaria

PHYLUM: Mollusca
CLASS: Bivalvia
ORDER: Unionoida
FAMILY: Unionidae
STATUS: Critically endangered, IUCN
Endangered, ESA
RANGE: USA (Alabama, Illinois, Indiana, Kentucky, Ohio, Tennessee, Virginia, West Virginia)

Fanshell
Cyprogenia stegaria

Description and biology

A medium-sized freshwater mussel, the fanshell measures about 3.2 inches (8.1 centimeters) long. Its shell is yellowish green with fine green lines across the surface. The inside of the shell is gray white. It feeds on plant material it removes from the water through a tube called a siphon. Muskrats are known predators of this mussel.

The reproductive cycle of the fanshell is complex. In the spring, a male releases sperm that is carried away by stream currents. A female takes in this sperm as she is feeding, and the eggs stored in her gills are fertilized. When the eggs hatch, the glochidia (pronounced glow-KID-ee-uh), or larval forms of the mussel, develop in the female's gills.

After a while, the glochidia are released from the gills into the stream. To passing fish, the glochidia look like worms. When fish swallow them, glochidia attach themselves to the gills (those glochidia that

Mussel, dwarf wedge
Alasmidonta heterodon

PHYLUM: Mollusca
CLASS: Bivalvia
ORDER: Unionoida
FAMILY: Unionidae
STATUS: Vulnerable, IUCN
Endangered, ESA
RANGE: USA (Connecticut, Mary-
land, Massachusetts, New Hampshire,
New Jersey, New York, North Carolina,
Pennsylvania, Vermont, Virginia)

Mussel, dwarf wedge
Alasmidonta heterodon

Description and biology

The dwarf wedge mussel (also spelled wedgemussel) is a very small mussel species. It does not grow any longer than 1.5 inches (3.8 centimeters). The outer side of its shell is dark in color; the inner part is much lighter. The mussel feeds on plankton (microscopic plants and small animals) and other plant matter it removes from the water through a tube called a siphon.

Like other mussels, the dwarf wedge mussel reproduces in a unique way. Males release sperm, which is carried by currents downstream. As they feed, females take in the sperm, which fertilizes the eggs stored in their gills. When the eggs hatch, the glochidia (pronounced glow-KID-ee-uh; larval forms of the mussel) continue to develop in the gills.

After a certain time, the glochidia are released and attach themselves to the gills or fins of a particular fish species. Those glochidia unable to attach themselves to a fish sink to the river bottom and die. In a few weeks, after having developed a shell, the young mussels detach from the fish and sink to the riverbed. There, they bury themselves, leaving only their shell margins (edges) and siphons exposed to strain the water for food.

Dwarf wedge mussels can use several species of fish as hosts. Among these are the tessellated darter (*Etheostoma olmstedi*), Johnny darter (*Etheostoma nigrum*), and mottled sculpin (*Cottus bairdi*).

Habitat and current distribution

Dwarf wedge mussels inhabit sandy and muddy bottoms of rivers where there is not much current and very little silt (mineral particles). Too much silt or sediment (sand and stones) in the water can clog a mussel's siphon and kill it.

The dwarf wedge mussel is found in 54 locations in 15 watersheds (areas of land where all water flows to the same place, such as a river) in the northeastern and north-central United States. The largest populations are in the Connecticut River watershed. North Carolina has the largest number of known sites. Today, however, most of the sites are home to only small and isolated populations.

History and conservation measures

The dwarf wedge mussel's total population size is uncertain, but scientists know it is shrinking. At one time dwarf wedge mussels were found as far north as the Petitcodiac River in New Brunswick, Canada. Now it is extinct in Canada, and populations farther south are becoming more isolated and spread over a smaller region.

All North American freshwater mussels face shrinking habitats because of dams and water pollution. Dams increase silt levels upstream; they also cause water levels, currents, and temperatures to change

Did You Know?

One of the major threats the dwarf wedge mussel faces is freshwater acidification (too much acid in the water). Acidification is responsible for the lack of minerals in many bodies of water. Although water becomes clearer and appears bluer when acidified, it loses much of its underwater life as a result of this lack of minerals.

Mussels survive by opening their shells and filtering the nutrients they consume. A decrease in freshwater nutrients leads to a decline of freshwater mussel species.

Acidification is linked to the burning of fossil fuels, such as gasoline, coal, and natural gas. When these fuels are burned, pollution is released into the air in the form of chemicals, which are brought back down into rivers and streams when it rains.

The dwarf wedge mussel is native to the creeks and streams of the eastern United States and Canada, where its habitat is threatened by pollution and disruptions to the flow of the waterways. COURTESY OF SUSI VONOETTINGEN/U.S. FISH AND WILDLIFE SERVICE.

downstream. Water pollution from industrial, residential, and agricultural waste is also a serious threat to mussel populations. Mussels have short life spans and need certain fish species to be able to reproduce. These factors make mussels especially vulnerable.

Although the dwarf wedge mussel is listed in the United States as federally endangered, conservationists (people who work to manage and protect nature) have raised concerns that none of the sites where it is found has been sufficiently protected. In 2003 the Nature Conservancy (a major environmental organization based in the United States) and the U.S. Army Corps of Engineers removed the Cuddebackville Dam in Cuddebackville, New York, to try to restore mussels and other aquatic life, but whether this tactic was successful has not yet been determined. The Nature Conservancy has also developed management agreements at sites in Vermont, New Hampshire, and Maryland. The U.S. Fish and Wildlife Service (USFWS) developed a recovery plan in 1993. In a 2007 evaluation of the plan, the USFWS found that some of the goals had been met but recommended creating protection strategies for some of the most important dwarf wedge mussel populations.

Mussel, fat pocketbook pearly
Potamilus capax

PHYLUM: Mollusca
CLASS: Bivalvia
ORDER: Unionoida
FAMILY: Unionidae
STATUS: Vulnerable, IUCN
Endangered, ESA
RANGE: USA (Arkansas, Illinois, Indiana, Kentucky, Louisiana, Mississippi, Missouri)

Mussel, fat pocketbook pearly
Potamilus capax

Description and biology

The fat pocketbook pearly mussel is a freshwater mussel that grows to about 4 to 5 inches (10 to 13 centimeters) long. It has a smooth and shiny yellow, tan, or brown outer shell that is round and inflated. In young mussels, the shell is thin, but in adults it is thick. The inside of the shell is pink at the center and bluish white toward the shell edges.

The fat pocketbook lives at the bottoms of large rivers in places where the water is less than 8 feet (2.4 meters) deep. It buries itself in the sand or mud at the bottom of the river with only its feeding siphons (tubular organs used to draw in fluids) exposed to the water. It then feeds by pumping water through its siphon, gathering nutrition from the tiny plant and animal life in the water.

The fat pocketbook spawns (produces eggs) in late August or September. To breed, the male fat pocketbook discharges his sperm into the

The fat pocketbook pearly mussel, once found throughout much of the Mississippi River and other nearby waterways, has seen its population drop and its habitat limited by dredging and other human activity. © COLLECTION OF THE ILLINOIS STATE MUSEUM.

river's current. The female, located downstream from the male, siphons the sperm to fertilize her eggs. The eggs are then kept in the female's gill (the organ used for obtaining oxygen from the water) pouches, where they develop into larvae (an immature stage of development, like the caterpillar stage of an insect). The larvae, called the glochidia (pronounced glow-KID-ee-uh), hatch in June or July, and the female fat pocketbook expels them into the water.

In order to survive, each larva must find a host fish and clamp onto it with its tiny clasping valves. Only certain fish, such as freshwater drum and white crappie, are suitable hosts for fat pocketbooks. If the larva does not find a host fish, it will fall to the bottom of the river and die. The larva that finds a host will remain attached to the fish for about two to four weeks, until it has grown its own shell. At that point, it unclasps itself from the fish and, if it is lucky enough to be in an appropriate habitat, buries itself in the sand or mud at the bottom of the river or stream. There it will probably remain for its long life. The life span of a fat pocketbook may be up to 50 years.

Habitat and current distribution

The fat pocketbook is found in drainage ditches or in sand, gravel, or muddy streams with flowing water. It lives in the lower Mississippi River, the Wabash and Ohio Rivers, the Cumberland River, the White River and St. Francis River in Arkansas, and tributaries (rivers or steams flowing into larger rivers or lakes) in Kentucky, Illinois, and Indiana.

History and conservation measures

The fat pocketbook became endangered due to severe loss of habitat. This occurred because humans have changed the course or nature of the waterways in which the fat pocketbook lives. This mussel lives in the sand or mud at the bottom of rivers, and dam construction and dredging (digging up the river bottom) changes the amount of this sand and mud. Biologists (people who study living organisms) must move mussels to new habitats when rivers are dredged. When the species was listed as endangered, biologists thought that siltation (pollution of water by particles of sand or clay) also harmed fat pocketbook mussels by blocking their feeding organs and suffocating them. Since then, biologists have discovered that this species of mussel can survive in silty areas where other mussel species cannot.

In 1989 the U.S. Fish and Wildlife Service put together a recovery plan for the fat pocketbook. It included protecting the population of the species living in the St. Francis River in Arkansas and finding and protecting two other healthy populations of the species in two different river systems in its historical range. By the 2010s the species' status had improved significantly. The main fat pocketbook populations in the St. Francis and lower Wabash Rivers were found to be healthy. The mussels can tolerate sedimentation (sand and clay particles that settle to the bottom) in the rivers. Biologists also discovered a large population in the Mississippi River. The species was believed to be doing well because flood control and dredging activities have slowed on the rivers where the mussels are found. Also, water discharged into these rivers became cleaner, thanks to several environmental laws. One new potential threat to the fat pocketbook, however, is the introduction of a nonnative species, the invasive zebra mussel, which could compete for food and habitat with the fat pocketbook and other native mollusks.

Although the fat pocketbook still maintained its endangered status in 2015 under the Endangered Species Act, the U.S. Fish and Wildlife Service said that if improvement continues, this species could soon be removed from the list. The International Union for Conservation of Nature and Natural Resources (IUCN) updated the status of the species from critically endangered to vulnerable in 2012 because the current populations seem stable.

Mussel, freshwater pearl
Margaritifera margaritifera

PHYLUM: Mollusca
CLASS: Bivalvia
ORDER: Unionoida
FAMILY: Margaritiferidae
STATUS: Endangered, IUCN
RANGE: Austria, Belgium, Czech Republic, Denmark, Finland, France, Germany, Ireland, Latvia, Luxembourg, Norway, Poland, Portugal, Russia, Spain, Sweden, United Kingdom

Mussel, freshwater pearl
Margaritifera margaritifera

Description and biology

Freshwater pearl mussels live in streams and rivers. They are bivalves, which means they have two shells attached together with a hinge. At the base of its shell, the mussel has a muscular projection called a foot. The foot helps the mussel burrow into sandy or muddy ground and anchor itself in place. The mussel can also use its foot to move slowly across the bottom of a body of water.

Pearl mussels are usually 4 to 5 inches (10 to 13 centimeters) long, although some can grow to 6.5 inches (17 centimeters) or can be as tiny as 0.4 inches (1 centimeter). Juveniles have thin, yellowish-brown shells; adult shells are thicker and glossy black.

Freshwater pearl mussels filter food from the surrounding water. Scientists are not sure exactly what they eat but suspect it is a mix of bacteria, plankton, fungal spores, and other organic matter found in freshwater.

Freshwater pearl mussels have disappeared from some areas due to the effects of water pollution and fishing. © LINDA PITKIN/2020VISION/NATURE PICTURE LIBRARY/CORBIS.

The mussels have a siphon, or tube, that draws in water. Its gills filter food from the water, and a second siphon discharges the filtered water out of its body. Juvenile mussels are preyed on by crayfish, eels, and the North American muskrat. The only predators that full-grown mussels have are humans, who harvest them for pearls.

The freshwater pearl mussel has a complicated life cycle. Adult mussels can be males, females, or hermaphrodites (beings with both male and female reproductive organs). Females may become hermaphrodites if they are in an area where there are not enough male mussels to reproduce. Males release sperm into the water in June and July. Between July and September, females, which have taken in the sperm through their siphons, give birth to larvae called glochidia (pronounced glow-KID-ee-uh), which are about 0.03 inches (0.7 millimeter) in length and have tiny, open shells.

The female gives birth by ejecting 1 million to 4 million larvae into the water over a period of one to two days. Most of these larvae die, providing food for other creatures. But a few encounter suitable passing fish, such as salmon or trout. The glochidia enter the fish's gills as it breathes. The larvae then hold on to the fish's gills by snapping their shells shut on them. This position gives them an ample supply of oxygen and food particles, and they grow and develop. By the next May or June, they drop off the fish and sink to the river or stream bottom.

Many mussels die at this point, as they fall on the wrong kind of stream bottom. But if a mussel drops onto clean gravel or sand, it will burrow in completely and begin the long process of growing into an adult. It takes 10 to 15 years for them to reach maturity.

Freshwater pearl mussels live a long time. Some have been known to survive for 200 years. Females are usually fertile for 75 years, during which time they can produce 200 million larvae.

Did You Know?

Pearls are formed by bivalve (two-shelled) mollusks, including oysters and mussels such as the freshwater pearl mussel. Natural pearls are created when small particles, such as grains of sand or bits of food, get caught between one of the bivalve's shells and a protective layer called the mantle, which covers the mollusk's organs.

The particle causes irritation. To stop this irritation, the mollusk secretes a layer of nacre to cover the particle. Nacre, or mother-of-pearl, is the same mineral that forms mollusk shells. Layers and layers of nacre are used to cover the particle, until a pearl is formed.

Pearl farmers are able to create pearls artificially by inserting a grain of sand into a mollusk by hand.

Habitat and current distribution

Freshwater pearl mussels live on streambeds in the Northern Hemisphere. They are primarily native to Europe, although they have been introduced in the United States and Canada.

By the end of the 20th century, freshwater pearl mussels occupied less than 5 percent of the range they had inhabited 100 years earlier. Adult mussels live for many years and are very hardy; many live in streams. Larvae and juveniles, however, are quite vulnerable. Scientists have found little evidence that juveniles and larvae are surviving or growing. Therefore, they fear that, without new growth, the mussels may disappear from much of their range in the first two decades of the 21st century.

History and conservation measures

Freshwater pearl mussels can produce lustrous (shiny), multicolored pearls. These pearls have been harvested by humans for thousands of years. As of 2000, pearl fishers have become a serious threat to freshwater pearl mussels in some parts of their range. The collection of mussels for pearls has contributed to the drastic decline of the species.

Mussels are also threatened by water pollution. The breaking down of pollutants uses up oxygen so that not enough remains to sustain life, including mussels. Juveniles and larvae are particularly hard hit.

Mussel populations are also reduced when pollution kills the species of fish that host mussel larvae or when the fish are forced to leave a polluted river or stream. The introduction of species that prey on or outcompete these fish also endanger mussel populations.

The harvesting of mussels for pearls is illegal in most parts of the mussels' range, but illegal collection still occurs. Conservationists (people who work to manage and protect nature) believe that the reintroduction of host fish species and controls on pollution are needed if the species is to recover. At the moment, however, the freshwater pearl mussel's long-term prospects look poor.

Mussel, ring pink
Obovaria retusa

PHYLUM: Mollusca
CLASS: Bivalvia
ORDER: Unionoida
FAMILY: Unionidae
STATUS: Critically endangered, IUCN
Endangered, ESA
RANGE: USA (Alabama, Kentucky,
Tennessee)

Mussel, ring pink
Obovaria retusa

Description and biology

The ring pink mussel, also known as the golf stick pearly mussel, is a medium-sized mussel, with a length of up to 4 inches (10 centimeters). The outer surface of its shell is yellow green to brown in color. Inside, its shell is dark purple with a white border. Adult ring pink mussels can live up to 50 years.

Like other freshwater mussels, the ring pink mussel breeds in a unique way. In the spring, males of the species release sperm, which is carried downstream by currents. As they are feeding, females take in this sperm, which fertilizes the eggs stored in their gills. Once the eggs hatch, the glochidia (pronounced glow-KID-ee-uh), or larval forms of the mussel, continue to develop in the gills.

After a while, the glochidia are released from the female's gills. They then attach themselves to the gills of a host fish (those glochidia that

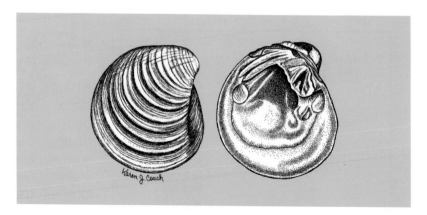

are unable to attach themselves sink to the river's bottom and die). The glochidia remain on the host fish until they have grown and developed a shell. Once they have, the young mussels detach from the fish and sink to the riverbed where they bury themselves in the sand, leaving only their shell margins (edges) and siphons exposed.

A siphon is a tube through which the mussel feeds, removing plankton (microscopic plants and small animals) and other plant matter from the water. Because this is the only way it feeds, a mussel requires a river environment where there is not much current and very little silt (mineral particles). Too much silt or sediment (sand and stones) in the water can clog a mussel's siphon and kill it.

Habitat and current distribution

The ring pink mussel is the most endangered of all North American freshwater mussels. Only five isolated populations of the mussel are known to still exist. They inhabit sections of the silt-free, sandy bottoms of the Tennessee, Cumberland, and Green Rivers in Tennessee, Kentucky, and Alabama. Biologists (people who study living organisms) are unsure of the total number of these mussels still in existence.

History and conservation measures

The ring pink mussel was once found in several major tributaries of the Ohio River. These stretched into Alabama, Illinois, Indiana, Kentucky, Ohio, Pennsylvania, Tennessee and West Virginia. As indicated by its current small range, this mussel is in grave danger of extinction.

Biologists believe the known remaining populations are all too old to reproduce.

As is the case with many other freshwater mussels, the ring pink mussel is disappearing because humans have tampered with its habitat. Dams built on rivers have caused upstream sections to become filled with silt. Downstream areas are subject to constantly changing currents, water levels, and water temperatures.

Water pollution is another major threat, especially to the remaining populations. Industrial waste and pesticide runoff (water that drains away, bringing substances with it) from farms are the main pollutants of the mussel's habitat. Oil and gas production threatens the Green River population of the mussel. Unless biologists discover new populations of the ring pink mussel in the wild, conservationists (people who work to manage and protect nature) believe that the future of this species is in doubt.

The U.S. Fish and Wildlife Service (USFWS) adopted a recovery plan for the ring pink mussel in 1991. The USFWS is conducting research to collect data needed to manage the species and to learn more about its habitat requirements, biology, and threats. It is also searching for additional populations and for suitable habitats where the mussel can be reintroduced.

Pearlymussel, little-wing
Pegias fabula

PHYLUM: Mollusca
CLASS: Bivalvia
ORDER: Unionoida
FAMILY: Unionidae
STATUS: Critically endangered, IUCN
Endangered, ESA
RANGE: USA (Kentucky, Tennessee, Virginia)

Pearlymussel, little-wing
Pegias fabula

Description and biology

The shell of the little-wing pearlymussel measures up to 1.5 inches (3.8 centimeters) long and 0.5 inches (1.3 centimeters) wide. The outer side is light green or yellow brown in color; the inner side is much lighter. Dark rays run along the shell's front edge. A white, chalky film often flakes off its surface. Like other freshwater mussels, the little-wing pearlymussel feeds on plankton (microscopic plants and small animals) and other plant matter it removes from the water through a siphon (a tube through which the mussel feeds).

The male little-wing pearlymussel releases sperm that is carried downstream by currents. While eating, a female takes in this sperm, which fertilizes eggs stored in her gills. The eggs hatch, and the glochidia (pronounced glow-KID-ee-uh), or larval forms of the mussel, continue to develop in her gills.

The pearlymussel's decline is linked to water pollution, especially toxic runoff from farms, strip mining operations, and industries.
COURTESY OF THE U.S. FISH AND WILDLIFE SERVICE.

After a certain period, the glochidia are released. Floating away, they attach themselves to the gills of a host fish (those glochidia unable to attach themselves sink to the bottom of the river and die). When they have grown and developed a shell, the young pearlymussels detach and fall to the riverbed. Here, they bury themselves, leaving only their shell margins (edges) and siphons exposed.

Habitat and current distribution

As of 2012 the little-wing pearlymussel was only known to exist in three sites in southeastern Kentucky, two sites in southeastern Virginia, and one site in central Tennessee. The species is very rare in its range, and the populations in the known sites are declining.

Little-wing pearlymussels inhabit rivers with cool waters and moderately to steeply inclined riverbeds. Because of the way the pearlymussel feeds, these rivers must have a low current and very little silt (mineral

The Manus Island tree snail's shell is prized by collectors. © LESLIE NEWMAN & ANDREW FLOWERS/SCIENCE SOURCE.

Admiralty Islands in Papua New Guinea. Biologists estimate that the number of Manus Island tree snails decreased 20 percent between 1998 and 2013.

The Manus Island tree snail prefers to inhabit the high canopy (uppermost layer) of the rain forests. During the day, it is mainly inactive. It is usually found about 16 feet (4.9 meters) above the ground attached to the underside of leaves of Dillenia and Astronia trees. It is also found on the leaves of large climbing plants.

History and conservation measures

The Manus Island tree snail's shell has been traditionally used by Manus Islanders in decorations and to create jewelry. In the past, large numbers of shells were either purchased by tourists or shell collectors. The snail is listed in Appendix II of the Convention on International Trade in

Endangered Species of Wild Fauna and Flora (CITES; an international treaty to protect wildlife), which limits international trade of its shell. The Manus Island tree snail was also the first invertebrate (animals with no backbone) to be protected under the U.S. Endangered Species Act.

Within Papua New Guinea, however, it is legal to sell the shells, and at one market on Manus Island it is estimated that 5,000 of the tree snail shells are sold per year. It is likely that some of these are illegally exported to other countries to be sold to collectors.

However, the primary threat to the snail is the destruction of its habitat because of logging, clearing of forests for rubber plantations, and road building. The trees the snail inhabits are valued for their timber. In the mid-2010s Manus Island was still largely covered in natural forest, but logging proposals have been made there. Conservationists (people who work to manage and protect nature) warn that if the large-scale removal of trees in the Manus Island tree snail's range takes place, reserves will have to be set aside to ensure the survival of this species. The forest habitat may also be threatened by the discovery of gold deposits that may result in mining operations.

Spinymussel, James River
Pleurobema collina

PHYLUM: Mollusca
CLASS: Bivalvia
ORDER: Unionoida
FAMILY: Unionidae
STATUS: Critically endangered, IUCN
Endangered, ESA
RANGE: USA (North Carolina, Virginia, and West Virginia)

Spinymussel, James River
Pleurobema collina

Description and biology

The James River spinymussel, also known as the Virginia spinymussel, is one of only three known freshwater spinymussels. These mussels are so-named because juveniles, or young, have one to three spines on each valve or shell. These spines are usually lost by the time the spinymussel reaches adulthood. An average adult is less than 3 inches (7.6 centimeters) in length. Spinymussels feed on plankton (microscopic plants and small animals) and other plant matter they strain from the water through a tube called a siphon.

The male James River spinymussel releases sperm, which is carried away by river currents. Downstream, females take in this sperm while feeding. The eggs stored in their gills are then fertilized. When the eggs hatch, the glochidia (pronounced glow-KID-ee-uh), or larval forms of the mussel, stay in the gills of the females and continue to develop.

A group of James River spinymussels is gathered during a population survey of a stream in southern Virginia. COURTESY OF U.S. FISH AND WILDLIFE SERVICE.

After a while, the glochidia are released into the river. They then attach themselves to the gills of a host fish (those glochidia that are unable to attach themselves float to the bottom of the river and die). When they have developed a shell and grown large enough to care for themselves, the young spinymussels detach from the host fish and sink to the riverbed. They bury themselves in the gravel or sand, leaving only their shell margins (edges) and siphons exposed.

Habitat and current distribution

This species of mussel is found in four headwater tributaries (streams that form the source of a river) of the James River in Virginia and West Virginia, and in the Dan River basin in North Carolina and Virginia.

The James River spinymussel prefers clean, slow-flowing freshwater streams. Too much silt (mineral particles) or sediment (sand and stones) in the water can clog the spinymussel's siphon, eventually killing it.

History and conservation measures

The James River spinymussel was discovered in 1836 in the Calfpasture River in Rockbridge County, Virginia. At the time, the spinymussel inhabited most of the area drained by the James River. Its current range is less than 10 percent of that original range.

A primary factor in the spinymussel's decline has been habitat destruction. Land adjacent to rivers and streams throughout its range has been developed into farms and urban areas. Runoff (water that drains away, bringing substances with it) from those farms, which includes insecticides, herbicides, and silt, poisons the spinymussel's habitat.

The James River spinymussel is further threatened by the Asian clam. This introduced species has taken over much of the spinymussel's former habitat. The Asian clam eats the majority of phytoplankton (microscopic aquatic plants) in the water, robbing the James River spinymussel and other native mussels of the nutrients they need.

The U.S. Fish and Wildlife Service (USFWS) adopted a recovery plan for the James River spinymussel in 1990. The service is conducting research to determine whether it may be possible to reestablish populations of the species in other areas of the James River. In addition, it is seeking ways to control invasive species (species from a different ecosystem that spread or multiply and cause harm when they are introduced into a new environment) that threaten the James River spinymussel, particularly the Asian clam. The USFWS has been coordinating surveys of the habitat area of the James River spinymussel since 2008 to monitor its population.

Critical Thinking Questions

1. Why might conservationists specializing in trying to protect a specific animal species have mixed feelings about that animal becoming downlisted (given a less endangered status) under the Endangered Species Act (ESA) or the Red List of the International Union for Conservation of Nature and Natural Resources (IUCN)?

2. Describe three reasons why it is important that species not become extinct. Consider possible effects on other species and on humans.

3. Some species face a greater risk of endangerment than others. What are some characteristics of species and their particular habitats that can lead to greater risks of extinction?

4. What are four effects that increased carbon dioxide emissions can have on the planet's climate and weather patterns? What are some of the impacts on living organisms?

5. Scientists have extracted DNA from the bodies of extinct animals such as the woolly mammoth and are exploring possible ways to use this DNA to create new animals, a process known as "de-extincting." Do you think this scientific pursuit is a good idea? Why or why not? Does your answer depend on which species would be "de-extincted"?

6. In 2012 the United States spent $1.7 billion to conserve endangered species. Do you think this investment is worthwhile? Why or why not? Is it too much or too little? (For comparison, consider that in 2015, the lowest state budget was $4.3 billion and the U.S. military budget was approximately $600 billion.)

7. Some conservation groups focus on a small number of endangered species that people find appealing. These "flagship species" include

into groups of six, each person taking a role representing a specific point of view, then debate whether the bird should be listed. The roles are:

1. A representative of a conservation group.
2. The head of an oil and gas company that plans to drill for oil and gas on land within the bird's habitat.
3. A rancher who grazes cattle on land within the bird's habitat.
4. A local birdwatcher who enjoys observing this bird in its habitat.
5. The governor of the state where the bird is found.
6. The government official who must make the decision whether to list the bird. (This person asks questions, makes a decision at the end of the debate, and explains why she or he made that decision.)

Once the debate is done, look up the case of the greater sage grouse online. How did the decision that was made balance these different interests?

4. Invent an Animal

Invent a new animal species—a mammal, bird, amphibian, or reptile that lives on land or in the sea. Write a description and draw a picture of the animal. Describe what it looks like; its habitat (air, land, water, climate) and how it has adapted to this environment; what it eats and how it protects itself against predators; its social behavior, reproduction, and care of its young. Is the animal endangered? If so, why?

5. Invite Others to Save a Species

In a small group, choose an animal or plant from *U•X•L Endangered Species, 3rd Edition*, that is not well known. Brainstorm and write down ideas for an advertising campaign educating people about this species and the need to preserve it. Create a slogan, think about which facts and issues you would emphasize, and discuss what kind of pictures you would choose to present. Consider ways to use social media, such as Facebook, Instagram, and Snapchat, in your campaign. For inspiration, look up World Wildlife Fund's campaigns online.

6. Inspire Awareness

Create a YouTube video for other students about an endangered species topic. You could focus on one of the reasons for endangerment (habitat loss, overexploitation, invasive species, climate change), a specific species, or ways people can help save endangered species.

7. Imagine Saving the Day

Create a comic book about endangerment of species. One option: create a superhero who tries to fight endangerment, villains who put species at risk, and animals to be rescued.

8. Examine the Five Deciding Factors

Some species are listed as endangered or threatened by the International Union for Conservation of Nature and Natural Resources (IUCN), but not under the Endangered Species Act (ESA). Examples include the addax, axolotl, European mink, Ganges River dolphin, giant sequoia, and Grand Cayman blue iguana. Look up the five factors for listing a species under the Endangered Species Act. Pick and research one of the six species listed above focusing on why it is at risk. Use *U•X•L Endangered Species, 3rd Edition*; the IUCN site; and at least two other sites as sources. Then, using the 5 factors, write an argument that this animal should—or should not—be listed under the ESA.

9. Explore Ecotourism: Pros and Cons

Ecotourism is a form of tourism in which people travel to natural areas to view wildlife and other aspects of the natural environment. It has some positive aspects, but also some negative ones. Research ecotourism and list the benefits and possible disadvantages of this practice. Describe some factors that should be considered in order for ecotourism to be done in a responsible way.

10. Evaluate Common and Endangered Animals

Many endangered animals resemble similar animals that are not endangered. In the United States, for example, the American bullfrog, black bear, whitetail deer, gray squirrel, and common garter snake are not at risk, but other species of bullfrog, bear, deer, squirrel, and garter snake are endangered or threatened under the Endangered Species Act. Pick one of the animals above, and on the U.S. Fish and Wildlife Service Endangered Species website, find the similar species that are endangered. Compare and contrast the common and endangered animals. Look at geographic ranges, adaptations, habitats, value to or relationship with humans, predators and prey, and other differences. Then, in a small

Resources (IUCN), which issues the official *Red List of Threatened Species*, describes 365 species on its list. Entries include reasons for endangerment, location maps, and photographs.

Kolbert, Elizabeth. *The Sixth Extinction: An Unnatural History*. New York: Henry Holt, 2014. Science writer Kolbert won the Pulitzer Prize for this book, which argues that humans' consumption of fossil fuels has led to a sixth period of widespread species extinctions paralleling the first five naturally caused extinction periods.

Mackay, Richard. *The Atlas of Endangered Species*, 3rd ed. Berkeley: University of California Press, 2008. A resource suitable for young adults and older readers, this atlas provides vital information on ecosystems, identifying wildlife, the importance of biodiversity, the transplanting of plants and animals across continents, and more. Also included in its 128 pages are case studies illustrating the major threats to biodiversity and the measures being taken to conserve the species.

McGavin, George. *Endangered: Wildlife on the Brink of Extinction*. Buffalo, NY: Firefly, 2006. This volume aimed at young adults explains that after five great extinction periods caused by natural events, human disregard for the environment is causing a sixth period of extinction. It describes endangered species and includes more than 400 photographs.

Montgomery, Sy. *Kakapo Rescue: Saving the World's Strangest Parrot*. New York: Houghton Mifflin Harcourt, 2010. Author Montgomery traveled to New Zealand to accompany biologists trying to save a critically endangered parrot species. It is part of the publisher's "Scientists in the Field" series, which includes books on many different animals, often endangered.

Neme, Laurel A. *Animal Investigators: How the World's First Wildlife Forensics Lab Is Solving Crimes and Saving Endangered Species*. New York: Simon & Schuster, 2009. Neme profiles a laboratory at the U.S. Fish and Wildlife Service where scientists use the bodies of animals to investigate wildlife crimes and curb trafficking in endangered species.

Pobst, Sandra. *National Geographic Investigates: Animals on the Edge*. Washington, DC: National Geographic, 2008. This short book for students ages 10 to 14 describes threats to animal species, outlines conservation efforts and what young people can do to help, and discusses formerly endangered animals now off the endangered species list.

Rogers, Kara. *The Quiet Extinction: Stories of North America's Rare and Endangered Plants*. Tucson: University of Arizona Press, 2015. Science writer Rogers explores why thousands of North American plants face possible extinction, why their survival is important, and how conservationists are working to save them.

Sartore, Joel. *Rare: Portraits of America's Endangered Species*. Washington, DC: National Geographic, 2010. National Geographic photographer Sartore presents haunting photographs of endangered animals and plants. The book is organized according to the size of the populations remaining of the photographed species, counting down to those on the edge of extinction.

Scardina, Julie, and Jeff Flocken. *Wildlife Heroes: 40 Leading Conservationists and the Animals They Are Committed to Saving.* Philadelphia: Running Press, 2012. This volume profiles 40 conservationists and the animal each works to save. Often in the conservationists' own words, entries reveal the backgrounds and experiences of these activists and describe the animals that are the focus of their efforts.

Turner, Pamela. *A Life in the Wild: George Schaller's Struggle to Save the Last Great Beasts.* New York: Farrar, Straus, and Giroux, 2008. Written for readers ages 10 to 14, this biography of noted biologist and conservationist Schaller explores his early life and his work studying gorillas and lions in Africa and tigers in India, among others. It richly describes the joys and challenges of studying endangered species in remote regions.

Watt, Simon. *The Ugly Animals: We Can't All Be Pandas.* Gloucestershire, UK: The History Press, 2014. Biologist and TV presenter Watt founded the Ugly Animal Preservation Society to humorously introduce endangered animals that are often ignored. His book features photographs and descriptions of animals such as the dromedary jumping-slug.

Periodicals

Endangered Species and Wetlands Report
P.O. Box 5393
Takoma Park, MD 20913
http://www.eswr.com/

Endangered Species Bulletin
U.S. Fish and Wildlife Service
Endangered Species
5275 Leesburg Pike
Falls Church, VA 22041
http://www.fws.gov/endangered/news/bulletin.html

World Wildlife
World Wildlife Fund
1250 24th St. NW
Washington, DC 20037
http://www.worldwildlife.org/magazine

Websites

Bagheera: An Education Website about Endangered Species and the Efforts to Save Them
www.bagheera.com/

BirdLife International
http://www.birdlife.org/

Convention on International Trade in Endangered Species of Flora and Fauna
www.cites.org

Defenders of Wildlife: Endangered Species Act 101
www.defenders.org/endangered-species-act/endangered-species-act

Defenders of Wildlife Kids' Planet: Especies Fact Sheets
www.kidsplanet.org/factsheets/map.html

Ecology: Ecology Global Network
www.ecology.com/

International Union for Conservation of Nature and Natural Resources
(IUCN) Red List of Threatened Species
www.iucn.org/about/work/programmes/species/our_work/the_iucn_red
_list

International Wild Cat Conservation Directory—Big Cats Wild Cats: Endangered Wild Cats
http://bigcatswildcats.com/endangered-wild-cats

Kids Discover Spotlight: Endangered Species
www.kidsdiscover.com/spotlight/endangered-species

National Geographic Education: Endangered Species
http://education.nationalgeographic.com/topics/endangered-species/

National Oceanic and Atmospheric Administration (NOAA) Fisheries: Endangered and Threatened Marine Species
www.nmfs.noaa.gov/pr/species/esa

Species in Pieces (online interactive exhibition)
http://species-in-pieces.com

University of Michigan: Animal Diversity Web
http://animaldiversity.org

U.S. Department of Agriculture: Threatened and Endangered Plants
http://plants.usda.gov/threat.html

U.S. Fish and Wildlife Service: Endangered Species
www.fws.gov/Endangered/index.html

Wildscreen Arkive
www.arkive.org

World Wildlife Fund: Wildfinder
www.worldwildlife.org/pages/wildfinder

The Xerces Society for Invertebrate Conservation: Endangered Species
www.xerces.org/endangered-species

Young People's Trust for the Environment: Endangered Animals of the World
https://ypte.org.uk/factsheets/endangered-animals-of-the-world/you-can
-help-too

Zoological Society of London: EDGE (Evolutionarily Distinct and Globally
   Endangered) of Existence
   www.edgeofexistence.org

Other Sources

Selected Organizations

*[Note: The following is an annotated compilation of organizations and advocacy
groups relevant to the topics found in* U•X•L Endangered Species, *3rd Edition.
Although the list is comprehensive, it is by no means exhaustive and is intended to
serve as a starting point for assembling further information. Gale, a part of Cengage
Learning, is not responsible for the accuracy of the addresses or the contents of the
websites, nor does it endorse any of the organizations listed.]*

African Wildlife Foundation
   Ngong Road, Karen
   P.O. Box 310, 00502
   Nairobi, Kenya
   Phone: +254 (0) 711 630 000
   Fax: +254 20 2765030

   U.S. office:
   1400 Sixteenth St. NW, Suite 120
   Washington, DC 20036
   Phone: (202) 939-3333
   Fax: (202) 939-3332
   Email: africanwildlife@awf.org
   Website: www.awf.org
   The African Wildlife Foundation is an organization that works to craft and
   deliver creative solutions for the long-term well-being of Africa's remarkable
   species and habitats. It also maintains offices in the Democratic Republic of
   the Congo, South Sudan, Tanzania, the United Kingdom, and Zambia.

Australian Marine Conservation Society
   P.O. Box 5815
   West End Queensland 4101
   Phone: +61 07-3846-6777
   Email: amcs@amcs.org.au
   Website: http://www.marineconservation.org.au/
   The Australian Marine Conservation Society is the only nonprofit Austra-
   lian organization focused exclusively on protecting ocean wildlife and hab-
   itats. It creates large marine national parks, promotes sustainable fishing,
   and protects threatened ocean animals such as sharks, seals, and whales. Its
   programs also combat climate change and reduce ocean pollution.

Australian Wildlife Conservancy
   P.O. Box 8070 Subiaco East
   Western Australia 6008
   Phone: +61 8-9380-9633

Email: info@australianwildlife.org
Website: http://www.australianwildlife.org/
Organized because Australia's animals face a particularly high extinction and endangerment rate, this nonprofit is Australia's largest private owner of conservation land, protecting endangered wildlife in 23 sanctuaries spanning more than 3.15 million hectares (7.78 million acres).

Bat Conservation International
P.O. Box 162603
Austin, TX 78716
Phone: (512) 327 9721
Website: www.batcon.org
Bat Conservation International works worldwide to save, conserve, and protect the 1,300 species of bats and their ecosystems, including 77 endangered species. Its approaches include preventing extinctions, protecting areas with large bat populations, addressing major threats to species, and sponsoring research.

Canadian Wildlife Federation
Ottawa—Head Office
c/o Customer Service
350 Michael Cowpland Dr.
Kanata, Ontario K2M 2W1
Phone: (800) 563-9453
Website: http://www.cwf-fcf.org/en/
This nonprofit's mission is to conserve and inspire the conservation of Canada's wildlife and habitats for the use and enjoyment of all. Its Endangered Species Program is the biggest nongovernmental source of funding to recover Canadian species at risk. The organization also produces TV programs, magazines, and books about species and sponsors programs encouraging people to experience nature firsthand.

Center for Biological Diversity
P.O. Box 710
Tucson, AZ 85702-0710
Phone: (520) 623-5252
Fax: (520) 623-9797
Email: center@biologicaldiversity.org
Website: www.biologicaldiversity.org
The Center for Biological Diversity is a nonprofit conservation organization dedicated to protecting biological diversity through science, law, policy advocacy, and creative media. By filing petitions and lawsuits, the Center has obtained endangered species status for more than 500 species.

Center for Plant Conservation, Inc.
P.O. Box 299
St. Louis, MO 63166-0299
Phone: (314) 577-9450
Fax: (314) 577-9465

Email: cpc@mobot.org
Website: www.centerforplantconservation.org/welcome.asp
The Center for Plant Conservation, Inc., is a national network of 39
botanical gardens and arboreta dedicated to the conservation and study of
rare and endangered U.S. plants.

Defenders of Wildlife
1130 17th St. NW
Washington, DC 20036
Phone: (202) 682-9400
Email: defenders@mail.defenders.org
Website: www.defenders.org
Defenders of Wildlife is a nonprofit organization that works to protect
and restore native species, habitats, ecosystems, and overall biological
diversity in North America.

Earth Island Institute
2150 Allston Way, Suite 460
Berkeley, CA 94704-1375
Phone: (510) 859-9100
Fax: (510) 859-9091
Website: www.earthisland.org/index.php
Earth Island Institute sponsors many environmental groups such as the
International Marine Mammal Project, the Urban Bird Foundation, and
Generation Waking Up, which involves young people in creating a sus-
tainable world. It also funds young conservationists and wetland conserva-
tion projects.

Earthjustice
500 California St., Suite 500
San Francisco, CA 94111
Phone: (800) 584-6460
Fax: (415) 217-2040
Email: info@earthjustice.org
Website: http://earthjustice.org
Founded in 1971 as Sierra Club Legal Defense Fund, Earthjustice is a
nonprofit law firm dedicated to protecting nature by working through the
courts. Earthjustice has played a leading role in developing environmental
law in the courtrooms and also in Washington, D.C., where it helps shape
policies and legislation.

Endangered Species Coalition
P.O. Box 65195
Washington, DC 20035
Phone: (240) 353-2765
Website: www.endangered.org
This nonprofit coalition of conservation, scientific, education, religious,
sporting, outdoor recreation, business, and community organizations
works to preserve and improve the Endangered Species Act. Its goals are to

end human-caused extinction of species in the United States, to safeguard animal and plant habitats, and to help endangered populations recover.

Endangered Species International (Headquarters)
2112 Hayes St.
San Francisco, CA 94117
Email: info@endangeredspeciesinternational.org
Website: www.endangeredspeciesinternational.org
This nonprofit focuses on species in the gravest danger of extinction, including those the media often ignores. It conducts scientific research about conservation, uses this research in projects worldwide, and builds relationships between governments, communities, and businesses.

Environmental Defense Fund
1875 Connecticut Ave. NW, Suite 600
Washington, DC 20009
Phone: (800) 684-3322
Website: www.edf.org
One of the world's largest environmental organizations, Environmental Defense Fund addresses Earth's most pressing environmental problems in the areas of climate, oceans, ecosystems, and health. It partners with businesses to craft solutions that help the planet while benefiting people economically.

Environmental Investigation Agency (EIA)
P.O. Box 53343
Washington, DC 20009
Phone: (202) 483-6621
Fax: (202) 986-8626
Email: info@eia-global.org
Website: http://eia-global.org
Environmental Investigation Agency is an international campaigning organization formed in 1989 that is committed to investigating and exposing environmental crime, often working undercover. One of the group's efforts is protecting endangered species by investigating illegal poaching and smuggling.

Fauna and Flora International
Jupiter House, 4th Floor
Station Road
Cambridge, CB1 2JD, United Kingdom
Phone: (202) 375-7766
Email: info@fauna-flora.org
Website: http://www.fauna-flora.org/
Founded in 1903, this British organization attempts to conserve threatened species and ecosystems worldwide, choosing sustainable, science-based solutions that take into account human needs. Its projects often focus on developing countries. It secures endangered species' habitats, monitors species' survival, and raises local awareness about species' impor-

tance. The group also works with businesses, partners with local organizations, and publishes a major conservation journal.

Foundation for Australia's Most Endangered Species, Ltd. (FAME)
P.O. Box 482
Mitcham, SA 5062 Australia
Phone +61 8-8374-1744
Email: fame@fame.org.au
Website: http://fame.org.au/
FAME is the only Australian organization completely focused on saving the more than 300 endangered species in that country. It works with other organizations, wildlife authorities, and private landowners and raises funds from individuals for specific projects, such as saving the mountain pygmy possum and the Tasmanian devil.

International Union for Conservation of Nature and Natural Resources (IUCN)
Rue Mauverney 28
1196 Gland, Switzerland
Phone: +41 (22) 999-0000
Fax: +41 (22) 999-0002

U.S. office:
1630 Connecticut Ave. NW, 3rd Floor
Washington, DC 20009
Phone: (202) 387-4826
Fax: (202) 387-4823
Website: www.iucn.org
An international independent body that promotes scientifically based action for the conservation of nature and for sustainable development. The Global Species Programme and the Species Survival Commission (SSC) of the IUCN publish a Red List online that describes threatened species of mammals, birds, reptiles, amphibians, fish, invertebrates, plants, and fungi.

National Audubon Society
225 Varick St.
New York, NY 10014
Phone: (212) 979-3000
Website: www.audubon.org
Audubon is a national network comprised of nearly 500 local chapters that are dedicated to the conservation and restoration of natural resources and focused on birds and their habitat. The group's work includes restoring habitats, operating nature centers and bird sanctuaries, and encouraging governmental policies that safeguard birds.

National Wildlife Federation
11100 Wildlife Center Dr.
Reston, VA 20190

Phone: (800)-822-9919
Website: www.nwf.org
This group works to protect U.S. wildlife and habitat for future generations, concentrating on safeguarding wildlife and ecosystems in an era of
climate change. It lobbies for environmentally sound policies and educates
the public about conservation.

Nature Conservancy
4245 North Fairfax Dr., Suite 100
Arlington, VA 22203-1606
Phone: (703) 841-5300
Website: www.nature.org
The Nature Conservancy is an international nonprofit organization com-
mitted to preserving biological diversity by protecting natural lands and
the life they harbor.

Oceana
1350 Connecticut Ave. NW, 5th Floor
Washington, DC 20036
Phone: (202) 833-3900
Fax: (202) 833-2070
Email: info@oceana.org
Website: http://oceana.org
Oceana, the world's largest international advocacy group focused solely on
ocean conservation, promotes policies that preserve the ocean's marine life.
Fighting overfishing and ocean pollution, members advocate for science-
based fishery management and restoring the world's oceans.

Wild Aid
744 Montgomery St., Suite 300
San Francisco, CA 94111
Phone: (415) 834-3174
Fax: (415) 834-1759
Website: www.wildaid.org
The goal of Wild Aid is to end the illegal wildlife trade by persuading
consumers not to buy products made from illegally caught animals and by
strengthening enforcement against capturing these animals. Its slogan is
"When the buying stops, the killing can too."

Wildlife Conservation Network
209 Mississippi St.
San Francisco, CA 94107
Phone: (415) 202-6380
Fax (415) 202-6381
Website: http://wildnet.org
Wildlife Conservation Network is a nonprofit that protects endangered
species in 24 countries by supporting independent conservationists with
innovative approaches that focus on work with local communities. The
group trains these activists and brings them together with donors.

Wildlife Conservation Society
2300 Southern Blvd.
Bronx, New York 10460
Phone: (718) 220-5100
Website: www.wcs.org
Founded in 1895 to protect the American bison, the nonprofit Wildlife
Conservation Society works to save wildlife and wild places worldwide,
managing more than 500 conservation projects. It is the parent organiza-
tion of the four major zoos and the aquarium in New York City.

Wildlife Preservation Canada
RR#5, 5420 Highway 6 North
Guelph, ON N1H 6J2
Phone: (800) 956-6608
Website: http://wildlifepreservation.ca/
This organization provides direct intervention with specific Canadian animals in grave danger of extinction. Its programs include captive breeding
and release, reintroduction of species, nest protection, and other interven-
tions. The organization focuses on preserving specific species, not just
protecting their habitats; it relies on well-designed scientific research and
hands-on work.

World Wildlife Fund, International (also called World Wide Fund for Nature)
Av. du Mont-Blanc
1196 Gland, Switzerland
Phone: +41 22 364 9111
Website: http://wwf.panda.org/

U.S. office:
1250 24th St. NW
Washington, DC 20037-1193
Phone: (202) 293-4800
Website: http://www.worldwildlife.org/
World Wildlife Fund works to address global threats to wildlife and
habitats. The group focuses on six areas: fighting climate change, feeding
the world sustainably, conserving forests, protecting freshwater habitats,
influencing policy worldwide, and supporting healthy oceans. Local offices
exist in many countries, including Australia, Brazil, Canada, Chile, China,
Fiji, France, Greece, India, Italy, Japan, Kenya, Malaysia, Mexico, Philippines, Peru, Romania, Russia, South Africa, Tanzania, Thailand, Turkey,
United Arab Emirates, and the United States.

The Xerces Society for Invertebrate Conservation
628 NE Broadway, Suite 200
Portland OR 97232
Phone: (855) 232-6639
Fax: (503) 233-6794
Email: info@xerces.org
Website: www.xerces.org

The Xerces Society for Invertebrate Conservation is dedicated to protecting and conserving invertebrates, animals such as butterflies and insects that are often ignored by other conservation groups. It advocates for policies protecting these animals, conducts research, and trains farmers and the public about invertebrate conservation.

Young People's Trust for the Environment
Suite 29, Yeovil Innovation Centre
Barracks Close, Copse Road
Yeovil, Somerset, UK BA22 8RN
Phone: +44 01935 385962
Website: https://ypte.org.uk
This British organization's goal is to help young people understand environmental issues, including wildlife endangerment, climate change, and threats to the ocean and rain forest. Its site includes educational materials, videos, and links.

Movies, Documentaries, and TV Miniseries
Arctic Tale (movie, National Geographic, 2007)
Born to Be Wild (movie, 2011)
Death of the Oceans (documentary, BBC, 2010)
EARTH: A New Wild (National Geographic series, 2015)
Frozen Planet (miniseries, BBC, 2011)
Last Lions (movie, National Geographic, 2011)
Life (miniseries, BBC, 2009)
Racing Extinction (documentary, 2015)

Apps
Endangered Species Finder (Android)
GeoEndangered (Apple)
Project Noah (Apple)
Species on the Edge (Apple)
Survival (game, free, Apple and Android)
WWF Together (Apple, Android, Kindle Fire)

General Index

B

C

D

F

M

S

Sage grouse, greater, *2:* 441
Sage grouse, Gunnison, *2:* **441–43**, 442 (ill.)
Saharan cypress, *3:* **684–86**, 685 (ill.)
Saiga, *1:* **225–27**, 226 (ill.)
Saiga tatarica, *1:* **225–27**, 226 (ill.)
Saiga tatarica mongolica, *1:* 227
Saimiri oerstedii, *1:* **168–70**, 169 (ill.)
Saimiri oerstedii citrinellus, *1:* 170
Saimiri oerstedii oerstedii, *1:* 169–70
Saint Barthélemy
    mahogany, American, *3:* **695–98**, 696 (ill.)
Saint Kitts and Nevis
    mahogany, American, *3:* **695–98**, 696 (ill.)
    plover, piping, *2:* **428–30**, 429 (ill.)
Saint Lucia
    mahogany, American, *3:* **695–98**, 696 (ill.)
    thrasher, white-breasted, *2:* **457–59**, 458 (ill.)
Saint Martin
    mahogany, American, *3:* **695–98**, 696 (ill.)
Saint Pierre and Miquelon
    eagle, bald, *2:* **332–35**, 333 (ill.)
    plover, piping, *2:* **428–30**, 429 (ill.)
Saint Vincent and the Grenadines
    mahogany, American, *3:* **695–98**, 696 (ill.)
Salamander, California tiger, *3:* **582–84**, 583 (ill.)
Salamander, Chinese giant, *3:* **585–87**, 586 (ill.)
Salamander, Texas blind, *3:* **588–91**, 589 (ill.)
Salmon, Danube, *3:* **629–31**, 630 (ill.)
Salvelinus confluentus, *3:* **657–60**, 659 (ill.)
Samoa
    coral, branching frogspawn, *3:* **601–4**, 602 (ill.)
San Joaquin leopard lizard, *3:* 779
Sandhill crane, *2:* 325
Sangoritan'i Belalanda, *3:* 757
Santa Catalina Island (Mexico)
    rattlesnake, Santa Catalina Island, *3:* **794–96**, 795 (ill.)
Santa Catalina Island rattlesnake, *3:* **794–96**, 795 (ill.)
São Miguel bullfinch, *2:* 303
Sarracenia oreophila, *3:* **713–15**, 714 (ill.)

Saudi Arabia
    dragon tree, Gabal Elba, *3:* **687–89**, 688 (ill.)
    dugong, *1:* **76–79**, 78 (ill.)
    ibis, northern bald, *2:* **372–75**, 373 (ill.)
    wolf, gray, *1:* **251–55**, 253 (ill.), 259, 261
Sawfish, largetooth, *3:* **632–34**, 633 (ill.)
Scimitar-horned oryx, *1:* **185–87**, 186 (ill.)
Sclerocactus mariposensis, *3:* 671
Sculpin, mottled, *2:* 545
Sculpin, pygmy, *3:* **635–37**, 636 (ill.)
Sea cat, *1:* 188
Sea cow, *1:* 76, 147
Sea lion, northern, *1:* 228
Sea lion, Steller, *1:* **228–30**, 229 (ill.)
Seahorse, Cape, *3:* 638
Seahorse, Knysna, *3:* **638–41**, 640 (ill.)
Seal, Hawaiian monk, *1:* **231–33**, 232 (ill.)
Senecio, *2:* 506–7
Senegal
    chimpanzee, *1:* **56–59**, 57 (ill.), 102, 106
    dog, African wild, *1:* **69–71**, 70 (ill.)
    eagle, martial, *2:* **336–38**, 337 (ill.)
    elephant, African, *1:* **84–87**, 85 (ill.), 88, 89, 90
    gazelle, dama, *1:* **99–101**, 100 (ill.)
    gull, Audouin's, *2:* **360–62**, 361 (ill.)
    oryx, scimitar-horned, *1:* **185–87**, 186 (ill.)
Sequoia, giant, *3:* **727–30**, 728 (ill.)
Sequoiadendron giganteum, *3:* **727–30**, 728 (ill.)
Serbia
    salmon, Danube, *3:* **629–31**, 630 (ill.)
    viper, meadow, *3:* **823–26**, 824 (ill.)
    wolf, gray, *1:* **251–55**, 253 (ill.), 259, 261
Setophaga kirtlandii, *2:* **470–73**, 471 (ill.)
Seychelles
    dugong, *1:* **76–79**, 78 (ill.)
    magpie-robin, Seychelles, *2:* **389–91**, 390 (ill.)
Seychelles magpie-robin, *2:* **389–91**, 390 (ill.)
Shark, Borneo, *3:* **642–44**
Shark, great hammerhead, *3:* **645–47**, 646 (ill.)
Shiny cowbird, *2:* 299
Short, Charles, *3:* 694
Shortnose sucker, *3:* **651–53**, 652 (ill.)
Short's goldenrod, *3:* **692–94**, 693 (ill.)
Short-tailed albatross, *2:* **293–96**, 295 (ill.)

T

W

X

Y

Z